Absinthe, Alewives & Alchemy

Kate Henriott Jauw

Ted Jauw

Copyright © 2019 Kate Henriott Jauw & Ted Jauw

All rights reserved.

ISBN-10: 1-7324304-1-1
ISBN-13: 978-1-7324304-1-9

'While Wormwood hath seed get a handful or twaine
To save against March, to make flea to refraine:
Where chamber is sweeped and Wormwood is strowne,
What saver is better (if physick be true)
For places infected than Wormwood and Rue?
It is a comfort for hart and the braine
And therefore to have it it is not in vaine.'

~ Thomas Tusser (1524-1580)

ACKNOWLEDGMENTS

Our journey and our story would not be possible without the amazing support of our family and our community. We are forever grateful to all those who have come before who have paved the way. We will continue to honor the sacrifices made, the love shared and strength given by all who have believed in us.

CHAPTER 1

Catherine knew she was asleep. Her eyes felt glued shut. She struggled to open them but it was so dark that it took her a second to realize it once they finally were open. As dark as it was, she knew that she was awake because she could hear sounds and she could smell smells and... No. These weren't awake sounds and the smell was like burning campfires and the sound was like, not 'like', it was... It was the oddly echoing sound of feet shuffling on sand. Dozens of feet going somewhere without any voices, without any other sound.

She felt herself being pulled towards the echoing of sandals on sand and she found herself in a room lit by torches. She quickly hid behind one of the several pillars that encircled the large round room. They appeared to be carved out of some sort of stone.

The impossibly large, smooth column felt cool and chalky. The feeling made her look at her hand for the first time and it was then that she realized they weren't hers. Yet, somehow, they were. The hands were smaller, darker and dirtier. They were a boy's hands. She wasn't sure why she thought this, except that she felt like a boy. Still herself but a boy and, oddly, not a boy. It occurred to her that she was seeing this through someone else's eyes, feeling this through someone else's body yet at the same time, it felt like her own. Was she dreaming?

She didn't have time to consider the answer as the sound of shuffling feet became shadows thrown by torches lining the halls that led to this giant stone room. Six doorways filled with light and shadows and, from the door directly across from him, a tall robed figure emerged with a torch.

The figure moved to light the six torches that were attached, one to each pillar. As the room brightened, she could see that the floor was not made from the same chalky stone as the room but was instead a mosaic of hexagonal tiles. They were arranged in a large hexagonal shape that emanated from a single hex-tile in the center of the room.

The center tile had a large cubed stone on it and she immediately understood (remembered?) it was called a 'cubit'. She also realized that she had one just like it outside of what she knew was the boy's own home. In the outdoor kitchen it was a place to grind, roll, knead and make things. Here, it seemed different. Sacred. Even though it was plain and empty. Really, no different than the one at his/her home but it felt like more than what it appeared to be.

When the torches were all lit, the figures, all hooded, filed in from the surrounding doors. It was T'Samhain, the moon before Winter Solstice, what some of the women gathered would call the eve of 'Omnia Consecrat' and the first snow had already lightly fallen the week before. Each figure that emerged from a specific door, wore the same robe as the one before. As the figures began assembling in a circle, she could see that each door's group had their own type of robe. Although the styles were the same, the materials were different as were their colors. Six different colors, cloths and, she noticed, coarseness. Six were fine like black velvet. Six like Red

Satin. Six a simpler dark Blue cloth. Six a dark green wool. Six were brown and coarse and the last six were white, like linen.

For some reason, the uniformity, solemnness and silence were making her afraid. She had the distinct sudden knowledge that she wasn't supposed to be there. She held her breath and shifted against the wall so that she could see more but still remain hidden in the shadow of the great pillar.

The figure who came in last wore a great bear skin, complete with the bear's head. She realized that this must be the leader, for when she dropped the fur that had been draped over her shoulders, it revealed a fine Indigo material, covered with embroidered stars. The great head on the bear that fell to the ground seemed to be staring straight at her now, with shiny glass black eyes.

The leader was a woman. Old, she knew, for these times, but young enough that her long hair was only beginning to gray. She wore no makeup or jewelry. Her long hair was straight and plain but shiny. She was beautiful, regal, and strangely sacred like a statue in a church on her pedestal, the cubit.

When she turned to look at everyone, she raised her hand signaling for all to drop their hoods and there, in one of the coarse brown robes standing and holding a torch, was his mother.

Seeing her there shocked him and he stepped sideways to hide behind the pillar. As he did so, the leader on the cubit dropped her hand. The women began to hum. Low at first, but it grew louder creating tones and harmonies that seemed to increase in intensity until it was what he could only describe as a 'thrum'.

He was still afraid that he would be caught, but he took comfort in the thrum as it echoed and amplified off the high vaulted ceiling and traveled back down the six portals. One voice in particular stood out to his ear, though it wasn't very loud. The melody he heard was his mother's song. The one she hummed at home. The one she used to rock him to sleep as a baby and the one she used to tuck him in still. It was the sound she hummed when her friends were over to help grind the wild wheats and the barley. The women would carefully pick the grains left after the men had harvested and the spicy hops, they dried on the rafters to make bier.

The familiar humming wasn't so much a melody as it was a series of weaving harmonies and the different melodies that the women made through their nose and mouth at the same time. Usually, it was calming but, sometimes, when the women at his house were angry or afraid, they would rock in a circle and combine their hums into a loud rope of harmony that could be heard far outside the simple daub and wattle cottages that most of them lived in. It could even be heard in the tiny wagon that he lived in nearby.

That hum was heard more often lately as it was rumored that 'Rome' was going to settle, once and for all, who ruled Helvetia. That is why it was so strange for him to see Roman Catholic nuns humming with Greek Byzantine nuns. His own family wasn't either. The locals called them 'Jennische' or 'Gyptienne' depending on whether they spoke Prussian or French. 'Helvetia', Catherine thought as she combined his thoughts with 'hers', what she called Switzerland. There was no Switzerland yet. The boy just thought of this place as a cave north of Lausanne. He didn't know he was in a 'Canton'. Just a place that was or wasn't a part of Rome, depending on who you asked.

If you asked these women, they would say it belonged to, first, the Snakes, then, to the Bears and now The Bees. The boy looked down at the mosaic tiles of earthy colored, muted tones decorated with mysterious symbols and runes. It was at that moment that he realized that his mother called her friends 'the hive' and she was called 'BeyKahtje' which meant 'little queen bee'.

The beautiful regal woman humming the loudest must be the 'big queen bee'. As he looked at the woman on the cubit, from behind his pillar, he swore that she made eye contact with him and he jumped back again. A nearly imperceptible smile crossed her lips and her eyelids dropped subtly. She knew he was there. She either didn't care or she was too busy to deal with a little boy who had somehow found his way into their giant hive.

So much was coming together in his brain as the hum crescendoed that he thought it would explode when suddenly… it stopped. Although he could momentarily still hear the remnants of the sound echoing down the halls, it became dead silent after only a few seconds. The women silently acknowledged one another with their eyes and with slight nods of recognition and respect.

The Bee Queen nodded to his mother and her head shifted slightly in his direction. Too late. His mother was looking directly at him and he was frozen by her gaze. She looked horrified.

She broke the silence and whispered, "What now?"

The Queen didn't hesitate. "We wait."

Her mother tried hard not to react. "I meant…" and she nodded in his direction.

The Queen Bee hesitated and said louder in Italian, probably for his ears, "The boy, Vano, must stay hidden and, hopefully, they won't find him."

He, Vano, did not like the sound of that. Neither did his mother, but the Queen Bee suddenly raised her hand and head. Everyone froze. Some women could hear what she could hear and others were straining. Vano was straining to hear too. His mother closed her eyes and a single tear coursed down her very still face.

K.L HENRIOTT-JAUW & TED JAUW

CHAPTER 2

Back in her bed, Catherine's body jumped as if she'd hit the ground hard after a fall. She inhaled sharply, quickly. "What the hell was that?" Her dreams were becoming more intense, more frequent, more real. She lay there for a few moments and focused on slowing her heart while trying to calm the, not butterflies, but seemingly large birds crowding and flapping in her stomach.

She put her mind to other things, like the laundry she had to do that day and the bit of cleaning. She wondered when her daughters would wake and clamor into the bedroom demanding breakfast. She was a bit surprised the dog was still sleeping and hadn't pushed his cold nose against her arm asking to be let outside. It must still be quite early.

The birds were talking outside, promising a good weather day. She tried to remember what game would be on tv later and hoped it wasn't one her husband was too 'into'. He tended to get very emotional while watching sports on t.v. and if his team didn't win, she would be walking on eggshells for the rest of the weekend. She was already dreading the inevitable outbursts.

After that dream, she knew there was no way she was going to go back to sleep. Resigning herself to what must be done, she slipped out of bed to let the dog out and make coffee.

As she was standing in the kitchen staring out of the window into the backyard, she had that increasingly familiar tingle and rush of energy through the top of her head. The kind that would often make her hair stand on end. It seemed to happen when she was worried or afraid. It seemed to be happening more and more. The increased pressure of trying to appear normal she thought might be finally getting to her.

The bark at the back door snapped her back from her thoughts. It also seemed to have awakened the kids. Damn, she was so hoping to get at least one cup of coffee in before the chaos. "Good morning, my beautiful people" she smiled as her daughters walked in the room.

"Morning" was the answer in sleepy little voices, then "What's for breakfast?"

"How about some chocolate chip pancakes?" After all, it was Saturday and she would try to make it a little bit special.

She was answered with a resounding "Yay!" and they ran off to watch cartoons while she pulled out the flour and the eggs. If it weren't for the sports on t.v. or church on Sundays, or the fact that her husband would be around all day, she thought she might rather enjoy the weekend. She sometimes felt guilty for wishing it were just herself, her girls and the dog alone in the house.

"Turn down the damn t.v.!"

He was awake. She still hadn't finished her first cup of coffee. She was tempted to interject a sarcastic "Good morning to you too!" but thought better of it and kept quiet. She was getting good at keeping quiet. Her husband would attribute it to her becoming a good Catholic at his insistence. Catherine attributed it to his decidedly un-Catholic behavior getting worse.

He entered the kitchen to pour some juice, as he was not a 'coffee kinda guy', and surveyed the bowl of batter along with the inevitable drips on the counter next to the pan on the stove. He noticed eggshells in the sink, "You better not let those go down the garbage disposal. They'll ruin it." Cat stifled the urge to roll her eyes. A glance to the sausages popping in the pan. "Why didn't you make bacon?" Then, "Are you putting chocolate chips in all the pancakes? I hate chocolate chips in pancakes."

She took a deep breath, then continued to calmly and artfully navigate the negativity all the while wondering if it was indeed too early to sneak a bit of brandy into her coffee. She knew it was important that he didn't lose it first thing in the morning, hopefully not at all. It was going to be a long weekend.

As she gingerly picked chocolate chips from the remaining batter, she thought, 'At least it was baseball season and not football' when he would constantly remind her, he was a high school all-star quarterback, and therefore, he was able to loudly judge that everyone else were idiots when it came to coaching and the plays.

The level of anger and yelling during football season was not a thing she relished. There was not the same level of attachment to baseball. Her Grandma had always liked baseball, well, the Cubs anyway. Her grandmother had been born in Illinois, near Chicago and had been a life-long fan. So, a bit of that was passed down and as her granddaughter, she felt that connection too. She was very thankful her husband hadn't completely ruined that much for her. She thought of her Grandma frequently, especially as the daffodils, were about to burst forth. Those had been her bulbs. In a way, it was as if her Grandmother still visited her each spring.

With breakfast over and dishes done, she started the laundry and did the sweeping. After lunch she and her girls headed outside to clean up the yard. Well, they mostly played while she raked up old leaves, checked on some sprouts, picked up twigs that had fallen throughout the long winter and dreamed of the herb garden she would plant some year. Maybe, this would finally be that year.

Her attention was pulled sharply back to reality when her youngest screamed and began to cry in a panicked manner. Crap, she thought, bees. Barefoot in the fresh clover blossoms was not the best idea. She shifted her brief thoughts of 'bad mom' guilt for not having prevented that, to remembering one of the 'weeds' she noticed beginning to grow along the edge of the patio was plantain.

She ran to it, grabbed a few of the new leaves and stuffed them in her mouth. She rushed back to her daughter while she quickly chewed, then took the spit filled blob of green out of her mouth, and pressed it onto the red and swollen spot growing on the bottom of her daughter's foot. She held it there with one hand while her other arm reached around the petite girl, scooping her up into her lap.

"It's gonna be okay, Marie. Give it just a minute" She said soothingly. Her big sister squatting next to them with a mixture of awe and disgust on her face, asked, "Are you a witch?"

The tingles rose sharply from the top of Catherine's head. She was about to answer when she was interrupted by yelling.

"What the hell is going on? What happened?"

Her husband rushed out of the house and knelt down to inspect what he was sure was mass carnage. Their daughter looked up at him and pulled back, closer, into her mother's chest. Instinctively, she held her daughter a little bit tighter. Her tears had stopped and she was feeling much better. The sting had subsided.

"It's okay, she accidentally stepped on a bee. But she's ok."

He was screaming. "Why the hell don't you ever watch where you're going?" Then to Catherine, "Why don't you ever make them wear shoes?"

Not waiting for an answer, his comment was followed with "Your mother is allergic to bees, maybe she's allergic to bees. We should take her to the hospital. What the hell is that crap on her foot? I'm in the middle of a god-damn game, I don't need this shit!"

Both children were visibly upset now and that nervous panicky feeling hit Catherine in the gut like a sucker punch. The dog moved between husband and wife, hackles up. It didn't go unnoticed.

"It's okay, go back to your game. I've got this." She wasn't sure if shutting him out was the right thing. But his kind of caring always came with anger and her instinct was to protect her daughters, always. He stood up with a scowl and stormed back into the house.

Later that night, after showers and baths. She playfully, tickled her girls as she chased them up the stairs. Their squeals and laughter got the dog barking, joining in the fun too. Which in turn caught the attention of their father who yelled at all of them to quiet down. Giggling, whispering and 'shushing' now, they all three, plus dog, jumped under the covers of her oldest daughters' bed.

At the age of eight, her oldest daughter, Stasia had already been devouring the 'Harry Potter Books' and was enthralled by the idea of witches and wizards. Which was much to the disapproval of her Catholic Church, her Catholic school and her Catholic husband. With the giggles having subsided, her daughter suddenly grew serious and whispered again, "Mom, are you a witch?"

All three grew quiet and, as Moms tend to do when they need to stall for time or don't know how to answer a question, she instead asked another. "Well...what do you think a witch is?"

"I'm not sure." Stasia paused thoughtfully for a moment, "I don't think it's quite like in 'Harry Potter' though. But you were just like Professor Sprout today. And sometimes, you're also kind of spooky." she giggled nervously at her own boldness.

Catherine laughed quietly, also a little bit nervously. "You think I'm spooky?" Keep answering with another question, she thought, how long could she keep this up?

"Well, you know stuff. Other moms don't know stuff like you do. You collect goddesses. Dad hates them but you still do it. Plus, you always know about dreams."

"And that's spooky to you?" She was getting good.

"I guess not 'spooky'. But it's different. Dad looks scared when you talk about stuff like that. I'm always afraid he'll get mad."

Head tingles again, and her gut pinched. She hated the thought of her children being scared. She worked so hard to try to make everything ok, to make everything 'safe'. She tried to smooth things over, protect them, hide them. She worked really hard to hide herself too." She added, "He hates that we're different."

Catherine lived in the suburbs of a very white, Christian town. She attended mass on Sundays. She dressed conservatively, brought snacks to her daughters' soccer games and the only people in the world who really knew who she was were her daughters. The three of them would always talk openly. They would leave food for the fairies in the wood behind their yard. They made magic wands out of the maple tree branches and set certain rocks out around their yard to act as guardians.

Since they had been born, she felt more inclined to reveal, or maybe relive all the magic she had embraced, in secret, during her own childhood. Her daughters' unconditional love and acceptance gave her the courage to explore and learn more about the magical world she had always been drawn to. She wished she had a place or a person she could go to so that she could ask questions and discover more.

She thought she couldn't be the only one who felt this. Although she didn't know anyone else who did. She began to consider that if she couldn't find what she needed, maybe she could create it.

Namely, she had been seriously considering opening her own shop. She dreamed of it. She would stock all the things she could never find in her conservative Midwest town. She knew these things could be purchased online, but wouldn't it be nice to have a place for people to go to? In person? The way she had always wanted to be able to do?

It would be a place where they could learn and explore their spirituality, ask questions, be safe. A place she always wished existed for her. She had so many questions, so many strange synchronicities. Maybe this would help her too. She decided she would carry herbs and oils and all sorts of witchy things.

Even with all of that, she never dared call herself a witch. That was a kind of commitment she wasn't sure she was ready for. As much as she was pulled toward what she thought of as witchcraft, she knew that labeling herself such, even in this day and age, wasn't quite a smart thing to do. And there was something else. Like a deja vu but from somewhere else, some when else...

"Mom?" She realized she had been lost in thought and couldn't think of another question with which to answer.

"Oh, my beautiful babies. I love you both so much. I guess, some people might call me a witch. You're right, Stasia, it's not quite like 'Harry Potter', but magic *is* real. Of that much I'm sure. Probably best if we keep this to ourselves for now though, okay?"

"Yeah." Marie, her youngest, piped in. Usually happy to let her big sister do the talking, she added, using the Harry Potter word for non-witches, "Cause Dad's a 'muggle'." It did not escape her that they saw themselves as witches too.

Quiet giggling ensued, hugs and kisses were given, Marie was carried off to her own bed, then lights out. She stood in the darkness at the top of the stairs. She wished she could stay in that moment forever. Listening to their even breathing as they slipped into sleep. She inexplicably felt the tears well up in her eyes. The sadness wrapped around her heart like the bittersweet vine she was forever trying to tear off of the big maple tree in the backyard. She dreaded the descent back to the living room. Back to a reality she just wasn't sure she could fake for much longer.

CHAPTER 3

Vano would not have to wait long to understand his mother's tear and fear. The tromping of too many matching marching 'boots', the boots that they called 'Caligae', echoed from far down the halls. Though far from Rome, Vano knew these soldiers were Roman Caligae, who still called themselves 'Militus Christi' or 'the Army of Christ'.

What he did not know was that they had ventured over the mountains for the purpose of coming to this very cave at this very time. As the 'Caligae', which was also the name they gave the soldiers, stopped suddenly, Vano heard a smaller group running toward the vault and suddenly every entrance was filled with the brown leather armor of Romans.

From the farthest entryway, a Centurion broke between the soldiers and, as he walked by Vanos' mother, ripped off her veil and pulled her to the central cubit by her hair. He never even looked at her but dragged her right to the Mother Superior who stepped calmly off the cubit to, still, look down at the leader of the soldiers.

He did not waste time and loudly yelled, "I accuse you of consorting with witches and practicing witchcraft with demons. How do you plea?" With this last sentence, he shook Vanos' mother by the hair with every word. Vano resisted the urge to run to her but his mother looked directly and sternly at him in warning.

The Mother Superior looked down at the shorter Centurion and she seemed to grow even taller. "It appears that you have already decided and come here as judge and jury as well. You know that as a Sister, I am a bride and also a soldier of the Christ, and I might add, unlike yourself, a Citizen of Rome?"

The Centurion had not expected any resistance and bristled. "You have till I count to ten and then we will commence killing." He looked around at his men. "On my command." he yelled loudly.

The Mother Superior suddenly began to speak to the Centurion in a different language. One that only he understood. "They sent you here because you are Paganis. You come here to kill a Roman for consorting with your own people?" She walked closer to him. He backed up. "Save your counting. I know how long it took you to learn it. If you wish to kill us, you'll have to kill me first."

Upon saying this, the Mother Superior suddenly swung a sword out from inside of her robes and cleanly cut the hair off Vanos' mother leaving a handful of it on the floor along with the Centurion's bloody thumb. He fell in shock and agony giving Vanos' mother a chance to escape while others closed ranks in front of her.

The women all produced short swords and circled the Mother Superior who now had her sword to the Centurions neck as he bellowed helplessly surrounded by two dozen armed women. Some women faced him as well with their own swords while others faced the soldiers at the doorways, who had their swords half-drawn but were afraid to move.

From the hallways, came the deafening sounds of women ululating with their tongues. The screams echoed so loudly that the soldiers were forced to take off their helmets as the high-pitched sound echoed in their heads. The hundred or so soldiers that had marched from their Alpen outpost were now surrounded by women of every size, shape and color, whose only commonality was the fact that they were all robed and armed.

The Mother Superior held the sword blade tight enough to the Centurion's neck that he could feel its sharpness. She spoke harshly in his native tongue, "Tell your men to lay down their arms or they will watch you die before we cut them to pieces. I assure you these 'witches' know how to butcher a piece of meat."

The Centurion yelled through gritted teeth for his men to stand down, while he held the stump where his thumb had been. He knew that the chances of him surviving this grew smaller as he realized he could not stem the flow of his own blood. He watched as his men dropped their swords.

As she let loose the pressure on his neck, she said something to one of the women in the Centurion's native tongue. When she came back, the woman in the rough robes produced a bunch of fresh herbs and proceeded to chew on it then grabbed the hand of the weakening Centurion. It was Vanos' mother.

She looked at the blood and wiped it with one hand then spit out the wad of chewed up weeds and placed it on the bleeding stump. Within a minute the bleeding stopped. The Centurion's eyes grew wide as she released the pressure on his hand. It was then that he fainted and the women took him away.

The Mother Superior looked out at the soldiers who were now stuck, huddled in each of the six hallways leading to the vault. They didn't know if their leader was healed or dead. She stepped back up on the cubit and looked around the circle. "I will let him live today and you with him. But only because you are all Paganus first and Christi Milite second." She used the Roman term for Soldiers of Christ that these men were sworn to be." She reached into her robe folds and pulled out her rosary that held a small black jet figure where the crucifix should have been.

"Behold your Mother." Most of the soldiers fell instantly to their knees and the rest soon followed. Some of them knew since they were Paganus soldiers from a Romanized outpost in the Alps, that no one from Rome would be coming to save them.

Back and still hidden in the dark shadows of the great pillar, Vanos had been transfixed for what had seemed like hours but it had really only been minutes. Only after the women outside the tunnels had safely led the soldiers away, his mother ran to him and held him tightly. She said nothing but he could feel her shaking once she realized that the danger was over.

"Come. We must go and figure out what to tell your father about why I cut my hair."

CHAPTER 4

Catherine brushed a non-existent hair from her eye out of habit. She had decided on a new look recently and had cut her hair much shorter. It was her attempt at trying to get her outside to match some of the inner changes she had begun to feel. It was a small attempt at trying to assert some control over her life.

She sometimes felt like she was just a trophy wife. Her husband would pick out her clothes. He would always comment on her body, hair and make-up, making sure she looked acceptable to him. Her new hair was seen as act of defiance. It was.

But she would still wear the clothes he bought her or wipe off the lipstick if it were too bright to suit him. She worked very hard at appearances and she did all the things she was expected to do, take care of the house, make the dinners, take care of the children, go to church. She even worked part time, again, to please her husband, who was never satisfied with the amount of money they had. She had become a suburban, blond, Republican, Catholic housewife.

Occasionally she would come across an old photo of herself wearing her funky thrift store finds, animal prints or with wild hair and she would wonder where that person had gone? But she wouldn't dwell on it too much and would, instead, convince herself that this is what she had always wanted, to be normal.

Doing all these things she thought were the right things to do, were supposed to make everybody happy. So, why did she always feel so sad? Worse, she was getting angry. She would put herself last, then blame others for not having the time to achieve her dreams. She was going to change this. By 'this' she meant 'everything'.

Starting a business would be one dream she would finally achieve but she was still scared to try. She was also scared to fail. But she was more afraid of never attempting to make her dream a reality and living with regrets. At the back of her mind she also knew that, if it worked, she would be financially secure enough to be able to leave her marriage.

All of the logical business things made great sense as talking points whenever she was questioned about her decision to open a shop. She wasn't sure what really drove her to continue. She just knew she had to do it, no matter how many forms and applications she had to fill out, as she was now doing. Her eyes started to glaze over and, she realized, she had re-read the same paragraph six times. She pushed back her chair and shifted her gaze to the window.

The sun was shining and it was very warm for that time of the year. She had about 2 hours left before she had to pick up her girls. "Screw it," she thought, "I'm going to sit outside".

She pulled on some shorts and a t-shirt and walked barefoot as she dragged a chaise lounge out into the yard. She unfolded it, tossed down a towel to keep from sticking to the plastic and laid back, closing her eyes to the warm sun.

It felt good to relax. Something she realized she never really did anymore. She always seemed to feel nervous, anxious, adrenalized and sad. The only time she felt 'normal' was when she envisioned her shop and dreamed of where that could take her. With so many details falling into place, she realized she still hadn't even come up with a name. Nothing sounded right. Her mind struggled with this even now she began to mull it over. She drifted as she thought, her thoughts drifted as she lay and though she wasn't asleep, she felt not quite awake either.

She heard the rustle of the grass as a Robin landed in it. She thought it a little strange that she could hear this detail as it was quite far away from her. She could 'see' the white glow around the plants in her garden and could swear she could hear them 'talking' to each other. They seemed to move on their own and not in conjunction with the slight breeze.

It reminded her of when she was little and used to 'eavesdrop' on the trees outside her window. She could hear their conversations and would take note that the sounds did not travel with the wind, but in their own direction, according to the conversation. She would lie in bed at night and try to predict from which direction there would come an answer. She was always right.

Even as an adult, trees were still special to her, especially the big Maple tree in her own backyard. After all the years of working to block such things out, she began to 'talk' to that tree and worked for a year to heal it from a fungus. That tree loved her daughters, she was sure of it. So were they, and they even took to calling him Grandpa. She felt as if he protected the house and, in his own way, her and her daughters, who were growing up like she did but with at least one parent who understood.

This time, however, as she listened for the trees to speak in their murmured way, she heard something else.

"Terra Stella".

"What?" She heard the woman's voice as clearly as if she had been standing right next to her. The tingles rushed out the top of her head as she asked whoever it was, "Is that Latin? Wait, who are you?" She immediately realized that there were two women there with her, she couldn't see them, but she could feel them, both.

"We are your Sisters."

"God" she thought, "My sisters?" She immediately felt a connection, a familiarity and then, a sense of loneliness. Why did she have to come back without them? Why was she here this time around all alone? Then the images came. She closed her eyes to 'see' them better and to try to see who was with her.

Instead, they showed her a cobblestone street in a busy city she sensed to be the 1700's. They stopped at a building with a wooden door. She glanced at the sign above it, noticing the iron work, how it cantilevered out from the side of the building. She noticed the word 'Shoppe' but didn't get a chance to see much more.

Inside there were herbs drying and little pots lined the shelves. There were candles, jars and bottles filled with all manner of things she knew to have been lovingly collected and blended. She took in as much as she could in the brief glimpses she was given.

Though they didn't speak to her too much more in words, they did in her understanding. They let her know that it was up to her to carry on what they couldn't. Somehow, the time was different now. She felt excited and uneasy simultaneously. When the images left and the head tingles stopped, she ran inside to look up the words 'Terra' and 'Stella'.

"Earth and Star". It was perfect. She wanted to carry the herbs and the teas, the medicines of the earth as well as the spirituality and the divinity of what one could only think of as 'from the stars'. They had given her the name. They had given her hope. But they had also tasked her somehow with something that felt just a little overwhelming and scary. Scary because it wasn't like an assignment but more like a promise she had made and now they had found her and intended for her to keep it.

Her nervousness and excitement were forgotten with a glance at the clock. School would be out soon, it was time to pick up her daughters. She 'put on' her public face, sighed and breathed in her last little moment of being real before she went out to face all the other soccer moms in the school's pick-up line.

CHAPTER 5

It was a long silent walk for Vanos as he and his mother left the cave with the hundreds of women who had shown up to surround the soldiers. The women quietly went their separate ways, mostly grouped by the fineness or roughness of their cloaks. Vanos and his mother were in the rough cloak group that split off from the main group to go into the woods on the outskirts of the nearby village where they lived.

Where they lived was more of an encampment than a village but it had been there since long before Vanos was born and maybe even long before his mother as well. The coarse cloaks of the women hid the brightly colored and layered clothes of the 'Gyptienne' or 'Jennische', as they were called by the town folk. They called themselves 'Oublier' or 'Forgotten'. Speaking a strange mixture of Hindi, Spanish, French and archaic Latin, Greek and some language heir tongue was like a living history of their travels.

They not only had their own language but they also had their own ways and though often mistaken for the Paganis Stregheria women, they had a tradition all of their own. Part of their ways was a strange culture of silence or profuse and demonstrative talking with nothing in between. The long walk home was in the silence.

It was not till they were home that Vanos' mother finally spoke and, even then, it wasn't until she locked the door of the little wagon they lived in, she made a fire in the little iron stove and put on some herbal tea. Both were noticeably relieved that her husband wasn't there. She secretly hoped that he was on a several day drunk and sleeping it off in some pub or even some whorehouse. As a blacksmith in town, he often forgot to make it home to his wife and child and for this, Vanos and his mother were grateful.

When she finally spoke, all she said was, "You are lucky to be alive." Vanos simply nodded as he watched his mother rinse blood out of her too short hair into a basin. He knew that his father would beat her for cutting her hair and he also knew that she would not tell him the truth of what happened.

As a Roma or what the locals called 'Gyptienne', he pretended to be 'Sicilian' to the town folk and treated his wife like the Romans treated theirs. Like property. As a husband and father, he was not really a presence in their life except to provide beatings which had become more frequent since Vanos had decided to be a boy instead of the girl as he was born and his father had wanted. This was not something that was unheard of but in his father's desperation to be accepted by the Romans, this was just one more reason to justify his violence.

Vanos' mother silently wrapped her head in a cloth but she knew she would have to uncover her head when she was in bed with her husband. As she quietly separated the fennel seeds, she had been drying from their stems, she looked at Vanos and knew that her beating would be followed by his. His had been getting worse. She suddenly stopped then and said, "Come. Help."

A few minutes later, they were hitching up the horses that they owned for pulling the blacksmith wagon. They used it to travel from town to town and, when the weather was nicer, she hitched it up to the old circus wagon that had traveled from far south of Rome and over the Alps almost a hundred and fifty years before. Most of the Jennische in their camp still practiced their acts for 'Fasnacht' carnivals and Vanos could juggle, walk on a rope and do magic, even though their little community had stopped pretending to be a circus many years before. But snake charmers, tea leaf readers and sellers of cures could still be found. Vanos' mother was known to be a reader or 'taffelteller', so called for the plate she used to contact the dead or to act as an oracle.

Vanos was a good horseman and the pure white horses were his best friends. If he weren't taking them with him, he would have refused to leave. Knowing they would be taking him to freedom and away from his father made him relieved and happy, despite his fear that his violent father would try to find them. Hopefully, he would not know they were gone until they were far away.

His mother didn't have to do or say anything as Vanos expertly hitched up the wagon while she tied a few belongings to the sides of their little house on wheels. Before she climbed up, she set down her riding whip, knelt down and touched the earth, touched her heart and reached up to the sky as if she were touching the moon and stars. She whispered the only Roman she knew, took off her Marriage scarf, wrapped it around a tiny 'sheaf' of wheat offering, and let it fall. She wouldn't need it anymore. And so she thanked the Mothers and the GrandMothers for her life.

Vanos watched silently and mouthed the words with her as he watched his mother repeat the Stregha Prayer she whispered just as her mother had before her. Vanos moved his lips in a silent whisper, "Terra Stella".

CHAPTER 6

Late at night after everything was done and she had fulfilled the expectations of her house-wifely duties, after her husband was asleep and her kids were tucked into bed, she began to work on her logo. She needed something to represent the earth and the stars. She also wanted shafts of wheat. Sheaves of wheat? Wheat was a universal symbol, for sure but she had some other personal feeling (memory?) associated with it. Those 'head tingles' she always felt when spirit seemed to be talking to her, now accompanied a gut feeling as she sketched each stalk for her logo.

The wheat could represent the Earth, the Terra, but also the harvest and the idea of wealth and abundance. That was what her mind rationalized as she drew but it was more than that. She just couldn't quite put her finger on it.

The other thing she 'knew' was that it had to include was a moon. She'd always loved the moon. She would feel less alone whenever the moon was out and about. On long car rides she would stare out of the backseat window and pretended that the moon was following her. It seemed that the moon was still watching over her.

When she was around 8 years old, she would sneak out at night and sit under the full moon hoping to get a 'moon-tan' which, she was convinced, would turn her skin into a lovely shade of silvery blue. With any luck, her hair would turn blue as well. She was always a bit disappointed the next morning to find that her skin was still pale and freckled and her hair the same boring blonde.

The moon was part of the heavens, but it wasn't a star and Stella meant star. Even though her vision for the shop wasn't fully formed, she knew what it would not be. There were already 'New Age shops in town and she had begun to realize that 'witchcraft', 'Pagan', 'Heathen' labels were not clear to her. She was still a practicing, if not believing, Catholic.

So, a five-pointed star was out and so was a six-pointed star. She felt drawn to a particular symbol of one with eight points. Was it supposed to represent Inanna like she had read about on the internet? Or maybe it was that dream...

She remembered a dream she had once in which she was guided to a large open room. In the middle of the room there was a stone pedestal. On top of the pedestal was a huge book. She walked to it and began to turn the pages. But as she turned them sand began to blow across the paper and when she brushed it away, the pages had turned to stone. On this stone tablet were strange carved markings. She ran her fingers over them frustrated that she could no longer remember how to read what it said.

After some research she found that same writing in a book about ancient Sumerians and read about the goddess Inanna. She began to read about a host of other Goddesses, all of whom were being tested by the fires or burned away to reveal their nakedness or even their skeletons.

There was something in Catherine that understood, she too would have to eventually bare herself completely in order for her to... What? She hoped Inanna's courage would show her.

The next morning, she took the sketch she had intuited to a sign shop and sent another sketch to the city for her permit to hang it outside the store once it was done. Later, she began to get ready for her evening. She had made plans to attend an open house at the Dominican Center in town. Every three months they would host an event showcasing all sorts of different alternative healing modalities. She'd heard about it for some time but only now had a chance to attend.

She always loved driving, and took her time now heading out to the convent. It was one of the few times she was alone. Sometimes she would blast the radio and sing loudly and obnoxiously to whatever songs she knew, then make up words to those she didn't. Today though, she was quiet. She pulled into the entrance and noticed the natural wetland area that stretched for several hundred yards before reaching the buildings. When she was about half way through them, she felt a distinct shift in energy. It was palpable, as if she were passing through an invisible wall.

Once through it, she felt an amazing sense of peace and calmness unlike anything else she had ever experienced. She wondered if the nuns had created a magic circle around the property? Then laughed at her impulsive thought of nuns casting a circle.

The place was much larger than she imagined. It reminded her a bit of a very small college campus. Not at all ornate or ancient like the churches she had once visited in Europe. Once she found the right place, she parked and headed inside and was greeted by a familiar voice. "Hey! Catherine!" She looked to see who it was.

It was Sister Susan, one of the nuns who taught Catechism at her church when Catherine was studying (struggling?) to convert to Catholicism. "I'd say it's a surprise to see you here, but I guess it's really not." Susan laughed.

Sister Susan had been a favorite of Catherine's. She had always made Catherine feel comfortable to ask questions and she never felt any judgement from her. Her demeanor was easy going and she was extremely knowledgeable about the Church and its history. "Of all my students, you're the one I would expect to be here. My only surprise is that it took you so long!"

Catherine smiled but wasn't sure what she meant by that.

"I remember you used to ask so many questions and challenge me at every turn. I could tell you were never quite satisfied with my answers. I could see you always thought there was more." She paused thoughtfully here as she worked out the best way to continue, if at all.

A year ago, she would not have hesitated but a new Pope had decided that Yoga, meditation and many other alternatives were satanic and the Dominicans, who had always been an open and 'alternative' order was on what her Mother Superior called the 'Stercus Album' or 'shit list' and they were awaiting the order to cease and desist. But this was not something that 'tertiary' or teaching sisters were allowed to discuss with the laity.

Instead, she said, "Maybe you'll yet discover what you were searching for."

"Are you teaching anything this evening?" Catherine asked. She loved listening to the sister who had a very different take on the Church than the ultra-conservative church that her husband insisted she attend. The self-same one that he rarely attended.

"Oh no, I was just opening up our bookstore and making sure it was all in order for this evening. But you go ahead and go on up. There are loads of interesting things happening." She gave Catherine a wink and a hug, said goodbye and wandered down the hall in the opposite direction. Catherine turned to decide where she would start.

It was set up like 'school' with a schedule listed on a board up front. Different mini classes were taking place at different times in various rooms throughout the building. There were things such as ear candling, Reiki, basics of energy work, use of essential oils in healing, working with chakras and beginning massage techniques. Catherine thought these were definitely not your ordinary sisters.

She went to the ear candling first. She wasn't so sure about this technique, the fire so close to a person's head and hair made her nervous. She tucked away the modality anyway. Although she didn't think this would be something she would do, or try on someone else.

The energy work was fun. The sisters had everyone pair up and face each other. It was then that she noticed she hadn't seen any men there. She didn't think it was a woman's only deal but she didn't mind, as her husband was a terribly jealous person and not having to partner up with a man took some pressure off of her.

They raised their hands so that their palms were facing the other woman's palms. Then they were asked to notice any feelings through the centers of their hands. Was it warm? Did it tingle? Maybe it felt like a wind? She could feel all three. The tingling movement, to her, seemed to radiate out in spirals but the wind felt like a column, almost solid.

She thought about her head tingles, gut feelings and her mother's hands when she would put them over a hurt spot when she was little. Her mother's hands used to get very hot and always made her feel better.

The last thing she had time to check out was the talk on the use of essential oils. She had always loved working with plants and oils.

Usually she mixed hers, but not always. She made a blend once to help soothe and heal the skin of a man going through radiation treatment. She used them in salves and in baths, on cuts and on bruises but she had never read about or studied oils.

This last class wasn't like learning. Even things she didn't know felt all too familiar. It felt like a memory. The nun had talked about the history of oils in her order and it, oddly, resonated with Catherine. She laughed as she thought of herself as a Catholic nun in a past life. Her head tingled as she said to herself, "Wait, we're Catholic. We don't believe in past lives." Then, she thought, "I don't really know what 'we' believe… or what 'we' are."

That last class ran a little longer than she thought. She felt the familiar panic rising in her stomach when she saw the time. "Crap", she thought. She was going to be late in getting home.

"Where the hell have you been?" was her husband's greeting upon her entering.

"I'm so sorry. It ran late. I lost track of time."

He launched right in. "Why? Who were you with?"

"Who was I with? I was with a bunch of Nuns! You know that! Anyway, it was an interesting time. It's really nice over there." She said, trying to change the subject while attempting to calm the fear rising in her stomach.

"Bullshit." He began to rage and shake. "If you wanna leave me, then leave. I know you're seeing someone else. But you'll never find anyone else who loves you like I do."

He stormed off, slamming the bedroom door. Thankfully, the kids were asleep. She listened a moment to make sure they hadn't heard and were awakened. She took a deep breath to calm her nerves.

Every time he raged, she felt all her insides roil and shake. His face was always so red, his jaw and fists clenched. She never really knew what was going to happen next. All her joy and excitement from the evening drained away. She kept trying to tell herself, "at least he doesn't drink, he doesn't do drugs and he hasn't ever hit me…" Yet. Was the word she left unspoken. She was tired of feeling this way. It wasn't right. She felt at a loss as to what to do.

She didn't understand. He was always angry. It wasn't like that in the beginning, was it? Was she that blind to the signs?

She remembered him seeming to change right after their first child was born. She remembered leaving her purse behind at the hospital after they had arrived home with the new baby. She was disoriented and emotional but he made her drive back by herself to get it because he refused to be seen carrying a woman's purse.

He had been angry and called her stupid for forgetting. When the nurses reacted in horror at the thought that she had driven herself back to the hospital, she was humiliated. She lied and said he was outside waiting for her. It was her first lie. It wouldn't be her last.

Instances like that seemed to gradually increase. His anger grew, his suspicions grew, his self-doubt grew and so did her excuses and lies. He seemed to change before her eyes, but maybe it was her eyes that were changing. Maybe that was who he had been all along. Maybe, to him, she was the one who seemed different.

Sometimes when he raged, she would flash to different times and places, even his face seemed to change into someone different, yet still familiar but always startling and disturbing.

Tonight had been one of those nights and she tried to push the thoughts from her mind. Instead she quietly walked down the hall to wash her face and brush her teeth. She even more quietly slipped into the bedroom to put on her pajamas.

He was turned away from her as he lay on his side of the bed. She gently climbed in, turning her back as well and stayed as close to the edge of the bed as she could manage without falling out. She thought if she didn't move and if she didn't breathe too loudly, he wouldn't start in again. Hopefully he would just go to sleep. Thankfully, that night, he did.

When she finally slept, she dreamt of a big bear. She was snuggled up to its back as they slept together in a cave. She could smell his fur as she wrapped her fingers around it and buried her face in the warmth. The dream gave her comfort. She found herself struggling to wake, not wanting to return to the world in which she lived.

CHAPTER 7

Her dream of bear felt like a gift after her dramatic dreams of the women in the "hive". It was as if the dream of the women still had a grip on her. She glanced at her hands first to make sure that she was still herself; her 'today' self. She quietly rolled over to check if her husband was there remembering the 'father' that the boy and his mother were afraid to return to. She unconsciously touched her hair in this lifetime and remembered how angry her husband was when she cut it without his permission.

She fumbled for her phone and was prepared to shut off her alarm when she noticed that there was a notification from the school. 'Don't forget! No school today due to conferences!'

She had forgotten. The kids would be happy and she would let them sleep in but she knew that he would be awake soon so she went down to make the bacon and eggs that he demanded every morning.

She made a pot of coffee for herself and placed it in a thermal carafe so he wouldn't see it. He sometimes got angry that she liked strong coffee as he did not, as if it was somehow a reflection on his manhood. It was one of many ways she would try to make sure he wouldn't notice certain things that might make him mad. She was terrified of conflict. There was always this strange feeling on the edges of her memory that something awful was going to happen if he got mad. She became an expert at avoiding conflict; and of convincing herself that there was nothing wrong with that. She had even started drinking more tea. She had always loved teas but strong coffee was what she needed to face the day. To face him.

She slipped on her Wellington boots and bundled up to go rake the leaves in the front yard. She decided to use the rake instead of the expensive mulcher her husband had bought for her as an anniversary present. She hated that thing, she hated the implication of what it meant and what it didn't mean. She felt angry and sad whenever she thought about it, even bitter. She was half tempted to use it and rob him of his last half hour of sleep. She decided instead, to not wake anyone and enjoy an hour of peace outside.

This would have the double effect of giving her some time alone and help her work off her anger about the night before. She wondered if she would have had the resolve of the mother in her dream. She sometimes wished she could just hitch up her suburban home to horses and drag it off to where he couldn't find her.

She was more 'shoveling' than raking the matted leaves from the previous fall. She began to scrape them from the sidewalk and considered clearing the neighbor's yard just to have a little more time outside when the garage door opened and her husband drove out into the dark without his lights on and without a nod or acknowledgement.

She stood still as he drove through her leaf pile and she hoped that he didn't see her in the dark street. Only after he had turned the corner, did she feel safe to walk back in. She sat down in her favorite chair still bundled against the cold air.

She watched the dirt and leaves melt off her Wellies and didn't care as they dripped onto the carpet. She had a feeling that she wouldn't be cleaning this carpet for much longer. She mumbled, 'fuck it' to no one in particular. As she stared at the last clump of dirt slide off of her boots, she felt her mind slide along with it, into another place and another time.

She saw the folds and drapes of long robes fastened together and watched as strong dark hands, (her hands?) slid out from beneath and clasp together in prayer. It was like a memory, except she was a man. She was in a cool dark room surrounded by dozens of terra cotta figures. They were all unpainted Madonnas holding babies. As she looked at her weathered hands, she saw that they were stained with reddish clay and realized that she was the one who had sculpted the figures.

She watched those hands as they reverently picked up little black 'figurine' pendants one by one. They were all less than a couple inches long and made of 'jet'. Not a stone but a petrified burnt wood that was so light it floated. The reproductions in her catalogues identified them as 'Venus' figures found in Switzerland. She looked at his workbench to see dozens of the black figures that had no head and large protruding buttocks that tapered to stylized feet.

Her hands chose one and she watched as it was pressed slowly into a rough piece of clay then she started working quickly to form the figure of a woman about eighteen inches tall with the small jet figurine hidden in the place of the 'heart'. A smaller jet figurine was then selected and again wrapped in clay and she watched as she quickly formed a smaller figure which she knew to be the baby. As she looked around, she realized that every figure had the tell-tale ochre stain of a jet 'Venus' within.

As she watched from her dream, Catherine realized that these were not really 'Venus' figures as her catalogue had described. The assumption that these were somehow sexualized, objectified fertility maidens was wrong. From the hands and eyes of the sculptor she knew that the little jet figurines represented menopausal 'grandmothers'. Their big butts imitated the fat that only old people would have accumulated 10-50,000 or so years before when doings and diets were different.

The black jet protruded a little from both the baby and the Madonna and she knew that this would be the 'couer d'alene' as the sculptor picked up an 'alene', an awl, and pierced the figure where the hole already was in the black jet. The hands then gently held out his own jet figure that was tethered to a leather cord and rubbed it in a piece of soft fur until it crackled and the hairs stood on end. He touched his figure to the little hole and a spark jumped from his figure to the hole. He covered it with a small ball of what she knew (remembered?) to be red ochre.

As she looked around, she imagined he must enact this ritual a dozen times a day as there were dozens and dozens of Madonna's with Child all around her in various stages of drying. She looked at the hands again and it went dark momentarily as he had once again clasped his hands together to pray. She realized that she was speaking Latin. Upon hearing it, she bristled and realized that her own reaction caused the sculptor to shake a bit himself.

The Latin had triggered an aversion she had developed because her husband had decided that they (she) needed to go to a conservative Catholic mass every Sunday and raise their kids in a conservative Catholic school. She had never felt comfortable there, even though she had gone through the conversion classes in an effort to try to convince herself it was what she wanted too.

She dutifully went every Sunday and listened to a young priest intone Latin in what she now realized was a tone deaf, terrible accent and pronunciation. As she heard the words come out of her own mouth she marveled at how melodious and beautiful it was and how it actually made her happy. In fact, she didn't want him to stop. When he finished praying, he went to the door of the studio, opened the top half of it and looked out onto the courtyard.

She looked out onto a walled compound as nuns and priests in simple robes the color of her own were busy as if getting ready to move. Crates and bags were piled outside of doors and wagons were being loaded. Under a tree, however, was an old woman raking leaves quietly into piles and shoveling them over where large wooden X's were erected and dug into the ground. A little boy grabbed leaves with his hands and followed the old woman to the X shaped structures. The old woman carefully fluffed each pile and scolded the boy for sitting in one. They were still wet from an early snow and she was trying to dry them.

Catherine looked at the little boy and thought 'Vanos!' with a quick inhalation but realized at the same time that the old woman was Vanos' mother. This boy would be too young to have been her son. Her grandson perhaps. The knowing came then, that she, Catherine, in fact, was Vanos, and the boy outside was 'his' son. She remembered, now, how this could be and she felt the man's motherly feelings as he/they watched the little boy play.

After watching for a moment, he turned slowly and proceeded to pick up the dried statuettes lining a wall on a long wooden table. He walked over to the kiln in the center of the courtyard and carefully placed the clay figures upside down in a careful stack near the oven entrance. He repeated this process and left space for the last dozen statues that he had made. They would be dry enough in a few days and he laid them in the empty space to dry in the kiln instead of on the tables.

He then began to load wood into the oven antechamber that would be baking these figures for the last time. As he looked out on the courtyard, he saw the little boy running toward him dragging a big burlap sack of dry leaves and he could feel himself tear up.

"Why are you crying, Papa?" It stung him that the little boy simply meant 'Papa' like he would to any priest in the little village parish enclave. He managed a smile and lied, "I will miss making these little statues." Then he hugged the little boy a little too tight and told the truth this time. "And I will miss you the most." As he grasped the well-worn jet goddess around his neck, he also held the crucifix that hung behind it and took off the necklace that all of the 'Brothers' wore and placed it around the little boy's neck. He took the little jet figure and rubbed it in the little boy's curly brown hair and touched it to his chest and watched the tiny spark jump onto the boy's heart.

The little boy wiped a tear from the priest's eye. "Papa, why don't you come with us?" The priest lied again and Catherine could feel his pain. "I must wait for the soldiers and go with them to Rome." He added, "Or whatever God has planned for me." That was less of a lie and he hugged the little boy one more time and sent him off saying, "Go help your mother, Andro, and make kindling piles."

As the little boy stuffed bags with the fallen branches of the many fruit trees planted there, the priest started to stack the kindling for the kiln, forgetting that he had meant to put the tinder leaves in the oven first. It struck him, as he looked at his little statues for the last time, that this would be the last firing of his handiwork before the Romans arrived to tie him to the X shaped crosses. Crosses that he himself had erected before they would burn him upside down, not unlike his little statues.

He went back to his studio for what would be the very last time and he gently packed what finished statues he had left knowing that they would go up north to Couvet to be painted into the Black Madonna's that the area was famous for. He thought it fitting that this little crate of black jet hiding Madonnas in disguise would travel, along with his last kiln load, in the wagon that he and his mother had escaped in and arrived here in, all those years ago.

As he loaded the crate into the wagon, he looked inside one more time. He saw the painted walls that were once a circus wagon and he looked at the Innamorati or the 'lovers' painted there. His birth name of 'Isabella' was drawn from these walls and his son's name 'Leandro' was also borrowed from these walls.

He inhaled deeply. Bags of Anise and Fennel seeds his mother had loaded onto the wagon filled the air and reminded him of her famous Dirgelli cookies, teas and elixirs that people would travel for miles to get even when they were ill. The recipes so old, they had come from Rome on this very wagon well before the Plague.

But to Father Vanos, they also smelled like his beloved. The priest who grew herbs in the healing garden smelled like Anise and Fennel as well as Sweet Melissa. He would have been the one to lovingly dry, then bag those seeds. Only now they were bagged to save them for another garden somewhere else and to send the secrets of their healing along with other secrets as well.

His son would never know that he was conceived in that wagon nor would he know that two of the 'fathers' about to be burned at the stake were his real parents. His son would also never know that his adopted mother and father were not really Italian and that his last name of Motta d'Dea or 'Fort of the Goddess', was not his adopted name but his, as his family had originally hailed from this lone Roman outpost of heretic priests that were about to be martyred for believing in 'd'Dea' or 'The Love of God'.

His fathers would carry these secrets to the grave, assuming that he would get a Christian burial, then only his mother would know the secrets that this little wagon had carried since the Plague ended a hundred or more years before.

As he looked at the wagon one last time, a hand slipped into his and the two priests turned back to the little fort that was to be their own final kiln. They exchanged a furtive glance to each other and looked back sadly as they walked away from the wagon that would carry their son to safety and touched each other's hearts one last time before they were seen by the others. As they let go and walked apart to gather more firewood for their own death, they both whispered, 'Terra Stella'.

CHAPTER 8

"Oh god!" she woke with a start. Her stomach was in knots, her heart was racing. Had she fallen asleep? Along with her sanity, she began to question how she was hiding in her own life. These images were all too real. She didn't understand or at least that's what she told herself.

"Hey, Mom, whatcha doing?" her youngest had just come down the stairs, rubbing the sleep from her eyes.

"Oh, I... just dozed off. I was up so early, too early, I guess. I needed just a few more winks." She forced a smile. "Hey you and your sis have conferences today. You're scheduled first for 2pm. We get to be lazy until then!"

She needed some "lazy". She had been busy with getting everything ready for the shop opening. She had finished painting the walls. She finished building the bookcase style shelving for displays, and was thankful she'd spent extra on renting a nail gun.

She was almost done with her mural of the trees and owl that was to be on the wall behind the front counter. She knew some people in certain traditions thought of owls as bad luck, or the bringers of death. But to her, it was her grandmother and it meant family and protection. She decided to write a portion of the 'Charge of the Goddess' there too, the part that said, "I am the beauty of the green earth, and the white moon among the stars". It was her favorite quote and really the only part of the famous 'rede' she understood. It was, hopefully, a reminder to all who entered that they too, were a part of the Goddess.

She was getting excited now that some of her ordered wares were coming in. She was waiting on a call back from the sign guy to confirm colors, but soon her sign would be finished too.

Today though, especially after last night and her dream this morning, she felt the need to simply hug her babies. Today she would take one moment at a time. It was hard because she couldn't wait for summer and school to be out and for what she then imagined, for her life to begin.

Her husband met her at the school for conferences. He didn't say anything to her, still hurt from the night before. She watched as his facial expression as it went from pinched childish pout to open friendly charm as Marie's teacher greeted them.

He was always 'on' when he needed to be. The perfect polite husband and father and she would play along, perfect wife and mother. It was easier, less risky that way. Afterall, this was how marriage worked, right? This was how it was supposed to be. At least that's what he always told her. Because he loved her so much.

It was always fun to go to conferences because both of her daughters did well in school. Especially at elementary age, there were often fun things happening. She loved to hear about their time in school. She was very proud of them both.

This time the teacher brought up her daughter Marie's latest project. The class was to bring in a food or item that represented their heritage and share about it with her class.

Marie and her mom had made Tirggel, a thin hard cookie from Switzerland, more of a biscuit really. It was made with lots of honey, various spices and rosewater. This gave them an opportunity to use the carved rolling pin her own mother had given her to press pictures into the dough.

While baking, Catherine told the story of the woman who had originally made this now famous cookie. "This is a very old recipe, you know. One woman who made it was a healer in a Swiss village way back in the 1400's. She was trying to help a very sick boy. He couldn't keep anything down, so she baked Tirggel for him."

They added honey, cinnamon, ginger, anise and more into a saucepan and she continued "The cookie was heavy on the honey to help fight the germs, the spices to soothe his stomach and intestines and the rosewater to calm his nervous system. Sadly, the boy was too far gone and she was not able to save him. But because she was the last one to have seen him and had given him something to eat, his family, in their overwhelming grief, accused her of witchcraft and of killing their boy."

She left out the part where the healer was put to death as a witch and finished, instead, with, "Incredibly, even after the boy died, everyone couldn't wait to get a taste of Tirggel!"

"What? Wow, Mom, that's crazy!" Marie interjected.

"I know! But the really crazy part was that after that, no woman was allowed to bake this cookie again, only male Bakers who belonged to Guilds in the city could produce them in their bakeries. And they made a lot of money on it too."

"That's not fair"

"I know baby. So much of life isn't. But we get to make it now, don't we?" then, a little more softly, remembering her dream, "It's different now."

"I just wanted to tell you what a nice report Marie gave us on Switzerland!" Her teacher gushed. "Everyone loved her cookies. Such an… unusual flavor." she added. Then, "I didn't know she was born there but I should have known by the way she pronounced the Tir… "She struggled to pronounce it and said, '…the cookie."

"Born where? In Switzerland?" Catherine asked.

"Yes!"

"Oh, no! She was born right here in the States" she answered with a slightly embarrassed laugh. "Kids! She must have been a little too excited about all of it." But Catherine thought, it wasn't excitement. Marie had memories and knowings just like she did. Sometimes, especially at her age, it was difficult to remember just what lifetime she was in. In fact, it was getting increasingly harder for Catherine to keep it all straight too.

She felt her husband cringe at the teacher's words. As if somehow his daughter's 'imagination' reflected poorly on him. But they made it through without further incident and left the conference with their picture and pretense of a loving family intact.

Once outside the classroom she was 'cold shouldered' again. For the most part, she didn't mind it but the silence left her with a gnawing dread, a nervous feeling in her gut, as she wondered when the next outburst would happen. She left him to get Stasia who was playing with friends and drop Marie at the playground. Stasia did not want to go to with her knowing that there was nothing she could do to please her father despite having very good grades.

Thankfully, Stasia's conference went smoothly. Nothing but praise from the teacher. It helped to assuage her father's fears of abnormality in 'his' family but he still couldn't stop from finding a way to make her feel bad even when she was doing good.

During dinner that night, Marie started to chuckle to herself. Both parents turned her way as her face lit up and she gushed, "Remember when you and dad were in the kitchen and dad dropped that big bag of flour and didn't realize there was a split in the end and it poofed up all over and covered your face and hair?! That was so funny!"

"That never happened! What the hell... I never did that." Her father was quick to answer and look accusingly at his wife as if this was some sort of proof she had been with another man.

Marie looked back at him, "That's 'because it wasn't *YOU*, dad."

'Oh shit', Catherine thought to herself, "I'm sorry baby, what are you talking about? I don't remember that." She responded, careful to not acknowledge or play into her husband's fears. Just recently, she had been getting better at 'talking' without words with Marie but not always.

Marie went on. "No, no, no. It was my *other* dad. From before. When I had my *other* sister and my brother, John." Then she added softly, "I really loved my brother, John."

They all sat quietly for an awkward second or two but, to Catherine, it seemed forever. She had been getting better at changing the energy in the room. Sometimes she just changed subjects. More often than not, it was by sheer will. Not this time.

Her daughter had just remembered a past life, she was sure. Again. To her husband, it was just one more thing to be paranoid about. All the women in his family seemed to be crazy, freaks and probably mentally unstable. Maybe even possessed. The only thing that kept him from being as hard on his youngest as he was on his oldest, was the fact that she liked sports. He had always wanted a son, so this seemed to be some sort of compromise.

But this didn't keep him from being angry that his oldest wanted to dress like a boy. Stasia, was different from the get go, walking at just nine months old and talking in complete sentences by thirteen months. She liked art, like Catherine did and drew pictures all the time. Often, she would pretend she was a fortune teller.

When she had been just four years old, she came to her mother in a sparkly dress-up princess costume holding an imaginary crystal ball and said "I'm a fortune teller! I will now tell you your fortune! "I predict...I predict..." she said while staring into her imaginary crystal, "that you and dad won't be together one day." She smiled and pranced away as if that was just a simple fact while leaving her mother sad and stunned.

After dinner she kept busy cleaning up the kitchen and getting her kids ready for bed while her husband retired to the living room to watch tabloid television or what he called 'the news'. They had school tomorrow and he had work, that meant she had some time to get some more things prepped for her shop opening. Which she had tentatively scheduled to happen in just two weeks' time.

CHAPTER 9

She sat down with her first morning cup of coffee and her long day's "to do" list laid out in front of her. Morning chores finished, she slipped into "business mode" and decided what to attack first.

She had been expecting a call back from the sign shop for some time now. She needed to confirm the colors so that the sign could be finished. She felt a little agitated in the delay and wondered what the problem was? Checking the time, she determined they would be open, so she picked up the phone and dialed the number.

"Hello Brian?", she inquired after the answer at the other end. "Catherine, with Terra Stella." She liked the way that sounded. "I'm inquiring about the sign for my store. I had been expecting a call but haven't heard anything. Is everything still on track?"

There was a pause at the other end and she felt those head tingles creep in. Something was up.

"Um, yeah. No. I was, um, actually thinking that maybe our shop isn't the right one to make your sign for you"

"What the hell? What did that mean?" she thought. She was totally caught off guard. He had already done the vinyl for the windows, the design for the overhead sign was approved by the city, she was hoping to install it next week. He wasn't the right one to make it? It was already made! It just needed to be painted!

"Are you serious?" was all she said.

"Look, I tried calling you back the other day. You weren't there. Your, uh… husband answered..." the pause told her everything.

"Oh god", she thought but said aloud instead, "I didn't realize, I never got the message."

"Sorry, I didn't have a chance to leave one. He hung up on me."

She said nothing at this but waited for him to continue.

"When he answered, I asked for you. He then began to yell and asked me who the hell I was? He asked why I was calling 'his wife', Told me I better stop 'fucking' you. I'm sorry, his words.

Then he told me I had better leave you alone or I would regret the day I ever met you. That's when he hung up on me." he paused, then added, "Maybe it's best we don't do business. I don't want to cause trouble."

"Shit, shit, shit", was all she could think. He had, in the past, kept his outbursts private, just between the two of them. She was used to him accusing her of having affairs. He had even accused her of having affairs with her girlfriends. But this was the first time he had accused someone else. A perfect stranger to him. And a business client! He was getting worse.

She was humiliated and panicked that she was going to lose this opportunity and investment. She was stunned into silence for what seemed like forever. Finally, she responded. Her tone now, less business like and more like the 'Cat' she used to be before her formal guards were up and she used her full name, 'Catherine'.

"Oh god, Brian. I'm so sorry. I really don't know what to say." She paused again and took a deep breath. She did know what to say. "Please know, obviously, this has nothing to do with you. I really need this sign. Don't quit on me. Call me on my cell phone from now on. It's almost done, it just needs to be painted right? Please. I'll make sure you don't have to deal with him again."

"Okay, yeah. Alright. I'll do it."

They finished up quickly and scheduled the sign for delivery the next week. She really didn't feel much like finishing the rest of her list. Instead, she went to microwave her now cold cup of coffee and stared out the kitchen window. She felt empty inside.

"Hey Mama" she said sadly to the spider who had taken up residence between the glass and the storm window. Although she was usually terrified of spiders, she left this one there as a sort of exposure therapy for her. She knew it couldn't get into the kitchen but it was still close and she would watch her and her habits, hoping that familiarity would not in fact breed contempt, but rather understanding and, hopefully, less fear.

So far it seemed to be working. No one else noticed her, so "no one" made her get rid of it, like he did when the snakes her daughters used to collect from the backyard got loose in the house or found their way onto the screened in porch. For being such a "tough guy" he really couldn't handle very much.

"Well, this has been kind of a sucky morning." She took her cup from the microwave carefully testing how hot it was before she sipped. "Did you hear all that?" she asked the spider. "Can you believe it? What shit..." Her heart ached with the pain and shame of humiliation, the truth of her relationship being exposed.

She sipped again and watched as the spider, who had finished cleaning up her old web, began to spin anew. She felt at such a loss, not knowing what to do. "What would you do?" she asked, laughing out loud when she imagined Spider's response, complete with affected accent, to be, "Well you know what we spiders do, darling, after we mate. Not much use for them after that."

But her smile faded as she continued to watch her friend thoughtfully for a few more minutes. The spider stopped spinning for a moment and seemed to look at her. Catherine noticed her eyes. Eight shiny black eyes, in each one a different lifetime, a different story, a different face, all hers reflecting back. This time she heard, "Clean up your mess, prepare something beautiful, attract what you desire. We are all connected. We will help." The head tingles returned, very strong this time.

"My mess." she repeated to herself. "Yeah, I guess it kinda is." She had hidden, avoided confrontation. And she chose time and time again to be quiet. She was always pretending to be someone she wasn't. She continuously rationalized and justified her actions or rather, her inactions. But now she was trying to become real, to grow, to live, to find happiness and her situation only worsened. She continued to push more and more against the constraints in her life. The more she pushed, the more he tried to stop her. This was not the life he had pictured, not what he had expected in a wife. The more she changed, the more he doubled down to stay the same.

She thought she was so brave to open her shop. But she knew deep down that even that was a kind of compromise. It was a way to legitimize her leanings, her interests and desire to learn more. Even through the store, she was trying to be all things to all people but never the one true thing to herself.

Standing there, lost in thought staring at the spider, she suddenly felt her grandmother standing in the kitchen with her. She could feel her love and support, she could almost feel her wrap her arms about her, spinning a web of protection.

Her grandmother had always seemed to know what to do. She knew how to take care of business. She had been a no-nonsense person and a trail-blazer in her own way. She was divorced, she owned her own business, she purchased her own home. She did things that were not so common for a woman to do in her time.

Now when she felt those familiar arms encircle her, she was less sure if it was a hug or a push. Maybe it was both. Either way, it was time for Catherine to spin a new reality.

"It's different now. It's different now. I'll be okay. This time I won't get killed." It was like some strange kind of mantra playing on a loop in her head. Although she knew they were her own thoughts, she didn't understand where they were coming from. But they were strong and they were insistent and they continued as if trying to convince herself to be brave and carry on.

She glanced back at the spider in the kitchen window. "No, not much use for them after that." she said remembering the spider's imagined response. Then thought, "Well, of course you kill your mate. Nothing personal right? If you didn't, he'd eat your babies." She knew she couldn't actually kill her husband, but the thought did make her smile. What she also knew, was that the store was one of her babies and she wasn't going to let it go without a fight.

She thought about her other babies then. She hoped that someday they would find themselves in a good and happy relationship. Then she thought about how mad she would be if they chose to live a lie, like she did. Her last thought was the realization that if this was the only example that they ever had, the odds of them doing just that were pretty damn good. And though she was still scared and she wouldn't say it out loud for several more months, in her heart she had decided. She was done.

CHAPTER 10

So many different people came through her shop as soon as she opened it. Many who were searching, some who were ill, some who were lonely and some who were curious. Some, more than a few, were just crazy. But even the crazy ones were welcome as long as they were respectful.

More often than not, her growing clientele was showing her that her life in the suburbs had sheltered her from a whole world of people. People who had alternative spiritual beliefs and alternative everything beliefs. Her shop was becoming a multicultural hotspot for those of all walks of life.

She was thrilled that several Christian ministers came in as well. Somehow, that signaled to her that she wasn't bad, she was still accepted. She suspected that her Dominican sisters were partly responsible. They came for censors or incense that they couldn't find elsewhere. Not at all concerned were they about the Hindu, Wiccan and Voodoo paraphernalia that also lined the shelves. And not a few black ministers who knew the difference between High John and Low John root also knew where to find her.

She enjoyed talking with them and answering their questions but also, she was learning. They were so unlike the group that came to stand across the street from her store with their bibles who prayed to have her demon soul banished and her shop closed.

The large variety of peoples that surrounded her daily in her shop made her husband very uncomfortable. He referred to her place as the Island of Misfit Toys. Perhaps they were misfits. But then, so was she. Just because she looked like a 'normal' didn't mean she was. But no matter who came through, what impressed her most was their 'realness'. Some that came through were more 'real' than she had ever known.

In addition to her regular clientele, she would occasionally be visited by the homeless, or neighborhood kids who had no place to go after school. Some visitors suffered from mental illness and depression. She began to realize that the real magic of her shop wasn't in the inventory that she carried. More stuff wasn't what these people needed. People needed each other. They needed to feel loved and accepted right where they were. She did too.

The young man who stopped in on this particular day had recently moved from Detroit. He introduced himself as Max and said he had wanted to meet the owner and check out the place. It had been recommended to him by her growing LGBTQ clientele. He was a practicing witch and had been working with a coven back home. Here, he was looking to connect and potentially teach.

She liked him immediately. He was young, smart, well-spoken and passionate about the craft. Plus, he worked with Isis and some others in the Egyptian pantheon and Isis had been more than poking around her consciousness for quite a while now. He talked about witchcraft like a 'craft' he was designing and not a religion.

They talked for some time. He had moved to the area, with his boyfriend, to be closer to his mom. Catherine agreed to schedule some workshops for him to develop. He decided on a sort of 'Wicca 101'.

Max was also an artist and, even though he had only lived in her small conservative town a short time, it wasn't long before her store had many new clients that were his many new friends and acquaintances. He already had lined up a gallery exhibition of his masks and she realized that it took someone from out of town to show her how sheltered she was.

Max's devotion to Isis was tattooed on his wrists. Isis seemed to have been speaking to her lately and when a Goddess talks, the only sensible thing to do is to listen. Max seemed to know Isis as someone other than an idol or even an Egyptian goddess. It was as if he had known Her in all of Her incarnations and guises and that was something that Catherine had never heard of. He even knew her ancient Catholic name and identity.

Although Max was teaching witchcraft through a 'Wicca' lens, a more recent witch 'religion', he didn't exactly practice that way. He freely used his own insight and discovery to create a more authentic way for him to express his craft, his own 'alchemy', as he termed it. This included knowing Isis in all her archetypes.

Isis first caught her attention as a statue in one of the catalogues she ordered from. She realized she didn't have any Egyptian Goddesses in her ever-growing collection so she decided to purchase Her. She had placed Her on the shelf at the store but realized that she couldn't let someone buy Her. She soon joined the mantle in her home with the other "Ladies" as she referred to the growing number of statues leaving her inventory.

But Isis was different. The others were beautiful or interesting but Isis seemed to be the one that always drew her in. One evening as she sat at the dinner table, she glanced over toward the fireplace and was startled to see that the disk in Isis' horned crown was glowing. It was strange and unsettling but she didn't dare say anything. Torn between keeping quiet and spilling her inner most thoughts she sat momentarily paralyzed. But Isis was talking, maybe she should too.

She decided that it was time. She had tried to talk with her husband before about her knowings, intuitions, beliefs and more. She did so now, reluctantly. She had finally decided to approach him again when she was at this very vulnerable but bursting point. She was emotional, at her wit's end and feeling scared at the awakenings happening within her. But even more at how he'd react.

Catherine couldn't hold it in anymore. In desperation, she tried to share what was going on inside of her, the dreams, the knowings, her doubts about what he wanted her to believe and even the fact that she was no longer the person he married, that she understood his anger at that but couldn't help it. The words spilled out of her in a rush so as not to lose her nerve.

He stood stiffly, quietly as she spoke, nervously baring her soul. When she finished, he just looked at her coldly, "I can see you probably want a hug right now. I just can't. You're kind of weirding me out." He stiffly turned his back and walked away. Now, she knew. Just as she 'knew' when she was a young girl. She should have remained quiet. This would only be used against her.

Isis continued to glow distractingly in the living room, she tried to divert her eyes and carry on as normal, as if nothing had happened, as if their exchange had not happened. Her heart hurt and she thought she had misread the signs. Afterall, inanimate objects, mass produced statues, do not suddenly come to life. Was she losing it?

"What the hell?" her husband suddenly yelled from the living room after walking out of the dining room and away from the unveiling of her heart. "What the hell is going on with your damn statue?"

"What are you talking about?" trying to act casual as possible.

"Jesus, it's glowing! What the hell is that, that thing?"

"Isis" she answered calmly but wasn't feeling calm at all on the inside. He could see it too. She wasn't crazy after all.

"Why is it doing that?" His voice was afraid.

"I've really no idea." she answered truthfully.

He looked at her in an almost paranoid manner. She tried to keep her gaze even so as not to give away the intense mix of feelings churning up through her gut and pushing on her heart. Though their eyes met only for a second or two, by the time they looked back to the statue, it had returned to its normal self. He looked back at her angrily this time, accusingly. She ignored his blaming stare, stood up and began clearing plates as if this type of phenomena happened every day. They didn't speak of it again.

About a week later another 'Isis' visited her in a dream. She was crouched in a cave. This Isis was sweaty, a bit dirty. Her hair was disheveled and she had an intensity about her that terrified Catherine. This was not the Isis of the hieroglyphs or the one she had seen depicted in art. She was not elegant nor was she bejeweled. She was the Isis of the caves.

This Isis was primal, maybe primordial, raw, naked, severe and passionate. The Goddess didn't speak but instead looked at her with growing intensity while She gathered together the severed, bloody limbs before Her. She was going to put them together again and she stared hard at Catherine as if to say, 'You can do this too'.

This was not the calm and regal Isis of her statue and, yet, it felt more familiar, more real and closer than any description or thing she had ever read. The dream was startling and, as it faded from her mind, she clearly heard the words, "Use your Magic". Then, she awoke with a start.

"Use your Magic? What the hell is that supposed to mean?" Catherine mumbled to herself upon waking. "I don't understand. Am I supposed to cast a spell or something, maybe to win the lottery so I can just run away from all of this?" She felt confused and a little bit angry. She felt amazingly 'unmagical' in the moment and overwhelmed with what she felt she had just been tasked. "Exactly how I am supposed to do that?"

She wasn't sure how or why, but the Isis from her dream was definitely working in her life right now. She knew she shouldn't question it. Sometimes in life, like those bloody body parts in her dream, things need to be completely ripped apart before you can begin to put them back together.

With Max's help, she began to unravel Isis as a complex mystery as if those many lifetimes were all working with her and some days, she felt like Isis the winged one, or Isis the one who was a snake and even the slightly less conservative and sexy Isis Aphrodite. She wasn't just putting the pieces together but she was finding that the puzzle had more parts than she knew and some other parts that had never belonged.

"That is a pretty intense dream." Max said after he heard about the Isis that showed herself to Catherine.

"Isis did have to reassemble and breathe life into her husband after he was killed by his brother. I guess it's your turn to reassemble and breathe life into...what?"

She was about to answer, 'not my husband' but thought better of it.

Max clasped his hands together then in a thoughtful repose. He was wearing a black shirt with a mandarin collar and Catherine momentarily thought he looked rather priest-like.

"What is it that has died in you?" he asked. "She told you to use your magic. Her magic is the Love of God, the teachings of healing, the blessings of life and of death. What is yours?"

"What do you mean Her magic is 'The Love of God'?"

"What? I didn't say that. I said Her magic is Love, of goddess, the teachings, healing and the blessings of life and death."

She didn't hear this last part either. Her mind had wandered as she noticed the faint scent of a lit match. But no one had lit a match. The smell grew more intense and, soon, it was the smell of fire long before matches were ever used. She had only leaned back in her chair for a second, but that was all it took to take her away…

ABSINTHE, ALEWIVES & ALCHEMY

CHAPTER 11

The old woman watched the melting ice from the entrance of the smoky cave. Every spring the women of the valley had watched carefully and awaited the prophesied time when the ice on the great lake would finally melt before the summer solstice. No one alive remembered the last time that had happened or, for that matter, the last time anyone had seen any of the beasts found on the walls of the caves. Only the bear survived. The cold that had driven away the great beasts had happened long ago but was still remembered, even if only on painted cave walls.

It had been so long since the big animals had roamed that most of the people of the valleys left long ago to follow what smaller game was left. Those that remained did so knowing that the ways of women were at an end. Their rule and ways as distant a memory as why great beasts were mysteriously painted on the cave walls.

In the lifetime of the old woman who now wore the Bear Robe, she could not count the number of women who had walked into the glaciers to die wearing only a coarse cloth and a necklace of the 'Seated One'. The 'Seated One' was a mother so ancient that she had no name or face. The only knowledge left of Her was that she was so old, she had once sat on the throne. Now, only the throne survived.

Today, the oldest woman stood looking out at the frozen lake, absently holding in her hand, her own 'Seated One'. It was now she who sat on that same throne and she who bemoaned the fact that she had not grown the large breasts or great buttocks of the GrandMothers of old. The days of women living old enough and long enough to develop the great bodies that showed that they had the privilege to sit on the throne, were gone. The only thing to remain now was the throne, the mysterious and unnaturally square stone of power called the Oracle Seat.

Despite her relative youth and lack of size, she was still Oracle and had prophesied at the solstice that the tiny little cluster of stars would appear after the ice melted on the great lake. She was wrong and the people were growing tired of her being wrong.

She had been known to have the 'gift' and, as those other women similarly gifted, died early or joined the others in taking 'the walk into the water' and drowning themselves, she knew what she must do. Some climbed barefoot into the glaciers in the hopes that an avalanche would take them and save them the indignity of having to dig their own grave. She knew that she had failed. That her gift had failed her. She had called down the Sun and the Lake was still a clean transparent sheet of ice as far as the Horizon.

She remembered as a child that the valleys around the caves held so many people that where she was now looking was filled with camp fires as far as the eye could see. Even in the Great Cold as they called it, there was enough game that no one felt the need to follow it to warmer places. Her atlatl was still good enough to take down a great buffalo or a wild oryx. But she had not seen any of those beasts since she was a maiden. A time when the great lake was smaller and farther away and slow herds still roamed the valley.

She had not seen an atlatl either in many years except on the altars. It was the bow and arrow that was needed now to take down the fast, little animals that still remained in the valleys. She saw, in her lifetime that men had made the bow and arrow a thing that only they could own and she watched her ways change as the men walked farther and farther away forcing their women and children to follow them or starve.

As the sun rose over the hills to the East, she already knew without having to look that the great lake was still frozen. No one had expected anything different. Except her. Now that it was confirmed, she went into the cave to prepare for what she must do. She would wake her young apprentice, before she left, to summon the women to gather. They would know what to do.

She herself went to the Great Seat and said her short prayers as she had, ever since she had become 'Oracle', the 'Seated One'. She went to a room where torches and other things were kept and she used her short bone knife to cut off a length of rope exactly two lengths of her outstretched arms. She went to the altars behind the large throne and picked up her stone plate and her little bag of bones. She carefully took one of the toe bones that had been rubbed on the stone throne until it resembled the throne itself. She left the others on the altar. She held her bone, stone and her precious share of rope.

She talked to no one, no one watched her leave, even though everyone knew she was leaving. As she walked out of the cave one last time, she dropped the great bear robe that would be given to one of the others. She prayed that whoever the bear chose to sit on the great seat would do better than she had been able to do. She knew too well that the people wanted her to tell them when the age of women would return.

It wouldn't. Not in her lifetime and not in thousands more. Maybe never. As she walked to the great lake, she shed the skins that kept her warm near its barren shore and when she had reached the lake's icy edge, she set down her stone and carefully unwrapped her feet then took off her last skin that gave her any warmth. She picked up her stone and walked barefoot onto the ice.

She walked out onto the frozen lake, never looking back. When she found a spot that was thin enough to see the blackwater underneath she laid her flat stone carefully on top of it and threw the little knucklebone one last time. She already knew the answer. She grabbed the knuckle and raised the stone plate above her head then brought it down hard to smash the ice in front of her.

She tied her rope in a cross around her stone, threaded it through the leather cord around her neck and rubbed the little carved 'seated one' in her long white hair one last time. She touched it to her bony sternum and felt the familiar prick that had given her comfort all of her life. She hugged tightly onto her little stone and hoped that she would not let it go until she reached the bottom. Then, like she had seen so many other women do in her long lifetime, she let herself fall through the hole in the ice.

As she sank, she said her last prayer. It was the only time that she had prayed anything other than 'I will...'. She made this, her last wish. A wish to see her Mother in the stars and to go home.

Before her wish was granted, she had one last vision. In her vision she saw that the age of Man would indeed end but only after 5000 suns were followed by 500 more and 50 after that then another 5. The Age of Women would not return but the Grandmothers promised to, if the Children were in danger and, as the old woman released her grip on the tiny cubit, it floated up and found its way to the small hole that had been broken into the ice.

A small hand grabbed it and, fist shivering wet, she held it tightly to her heart and ran back to shore. She gathered the furs and wraps left there, her only inheritance and walked back to the great cave where she saw the women of the Valley were gathering. She would not be allowed to enter to hear the 'Oracle' as the new one was seated but she decided she had all the answers needed when she had clearly heard that her grandmother would return.

CHAPTER 12

Catherine already spent a lot of time in her shop. Adding regular workshops after hours meant spending even more time there. She would drop her kids off at school, then drive into town and arrive around 8:30 am. She would clean, do paperwork, then open at 10am. She would have to close for an hour in the afternoon to pick up her girls, then they would all return together and hang out until 6pm. Hosting an afterhours workshop would make for a long day. But she figured it would be worth it in the long run.

She had set up the back room with a pull-out bed, a t.v. and an Xbox for her daughters. They would do their homework and eat at the counter up front. Sometimes she would bring her dog in too. It was a cozy arrangement that seemed to be working out. The kids were great there, though sometimes she knew they'd rather be at home. For the most part, they had a lot of fun. And they could always be bribed with a coke 'Icee' on the way in.

As for Catherine, she was grateful to have worked it out so that they could stay with her in the afternoons. She also very much enjoyed her morning alone time between arrival and opening. Although occasionally she would unlock the front doors early. In fact, it was just such a morning when a man walked in who would change her life forever.

She had arrived around twenty minutes past eight o'clock that morning. Still disturbed by an early morning dream in which she was drowning, she put on a pot of coffee that she would share with her patrons. Most of her 'busy' work she had finished the day before so she decided that she may as well open up, though she didn't really expect anyone that early in the morning.

She was behind the counter and noticed a car pull up in front. A man exited from the passenger side and stepped out onto the sidewalk. The car drove away and he stood for a moment with his back to her shop window.

He seemed to be getting his bearings as she watched him slowly turn to his right and look down the street. He glanced and took note of the display in her window. He looked up to the shop name above the door, glanced at the 'open' sign and walked in.

"Good morning" She greeted him with a smile.

"Good morning!"

He seemed pleasant enough. She still stayed behind the counter though. It was an automatic thing she did, like so many of her strategies that had become a habit of survival, particularly around men. She had been hit on so many times, groped, commented on, not taken seriously, put down, threatened and as a result, she thought about her every move.

She had learned to energetically keep a formality about her, a bit of a coldness and distance so that no one could ever accuse her of "asking for it". Not that it ever really seemed to make too much of a difference. She had also learned to physically, stay behind the counter, next to her "panic" button that would alert the security company should anything really bad happen.

She didn't feel him as a threat, though she remained wary. Better to be safe, as it was early morning and no one else was around.

He glanced around the store but didn't seem to be too interested in 'stuff'. She offered him a cup of coffee and he pulled a tall chair up to the counter.

"I don't recall this store being here. Have you been open long?"

"Oh, not too long now. It's only been a few of months."

"Ah, ok. I used to live around here but I've been in the Black Hills and California for some time now. I just moved back last week."

They continued their conversation until well past the shop's actual opening time. By that point, she had moved around next to him, pulled up the other chair and joined him for another cup of coffee. His name was Theo DeMott. Cat told him he looked too 'exotic' for a Dutch name like that. He laughed and quipped that his ancestors were 'Dark Dutch'. He had a warm self-deprecating sense of humor. He explained, 'Really, I'm Dutch Indonesian. The Dutch side were Sinti or what some called 'Gypsies', brought to the Terps of Holland to train their famous horses." He seemed to be a storyteller but she wasn't sure if that was good or bad.

She learned that he had been divorced for many years and had three children of his own. He had lived among and learned from Native North and Central American medicine people, African priests, Buddhists, Jungians and more. He had a degree in Paleontology and was versed in philosophy and poetry. He was also a Yoruba Diviner and Mayan Tarot reader and thought her shop may be a place where he would be able to offer that to the public.

He offered to give her a reading so she could see for herself whether or not he was any good. They scheduled one for a couple of days later. On his way out, he noticed her logo on a brochure on the front counter. He stared at it quietly for a moment.

"You have an eight-pointed star as part of your logo." he seemingly said as much to himself as he did her. "Why did you choose that?"

"The star is for the "Stella" part of "Terra Stella", but I chose that one in particular because of the story of the goddess, Inanna and her descent into the underworld."

"Are you familiar with the story of the Star Maiden?" he asked.

"No, I'm afraid I've never heard of that."

"She's like Isis and… Oh, well, another time I'll tell you… It's just that…" he paused thoughtfully, "one of my teachers once told me before she left that if I was to see this 'shield', I would know the person carrying it was one of my tribe."

And there it was, she thought. The absolute worst pick up line she had ever heard. Damn, and he seemed so nice and polite. But she was nice and polite, so she just smiled and agreed to keep their said appointment for the reading later that week.

CHAPTER 13

Catherine spent the rest of that afternoon thinking about the morning and the conversation had reminded her of Isis in all her various forms. She would have to pick up the girls in a few hours. It was January, so she didn't really expect too much traffic in the store. She thought she would go into the back and look at some catalogues. Max had given her a whole list of other names for Isis and she thought she would see if there were any statues she could add to her inventory.

As a new store, many makers, distributors and more wanted to make a steady customer out of her so she thought she might take advantage of the 'first order' deals coming her way. As she looked at the catalogues, she saw that most of the statues were cheesy and that the ones she liked were pretty pricey. She decided that her tastes were entirely too expensive.

As she looked at a catalogue of museum reproductions, she saw Isis as a bird, a scorpion, as a hyena and more. Then she stopped her thumbing and was stunned by a particular image. Here was an interpretation of Isis, sitting and nursing her son. No fancy wings, no jewelry, just a simple mortal woman nursing her son. She read the words underneath and it said 'Au Set' or 'female of the throne'. She had heard this name before but it was always 'Queen of the

Throne' and she was always bejeweled and crowned in the fanciest headdresses and sitting on the grandest of thrones. But here she was as quite an ordinary mom doing a quite ordinary thing. If nursing a god can be thought of as ordinary. She looked at the throne and was stunned. It was a simple stone block. Just like from her dream. The 'Seated One'...

She stood up to research this on her computer but did so too quickly and got dizzy. She sat back down immediately on her little couch but it did not stop the sensation of falling.

She was not falling so much as she was drowning. She felt both inside her body and outside of it as she watched herself slowly sink. She was holding her stone and could see the hole in the ice above her grow farther and farther away.

As she slowly lost herself, she remembered seeing a silhouette darken the last bit of light shining through the hole in the ice and she let out a little sound that became only bubbles in the blackness. She forgot that she was drowning and had tried to tell her granddaughter that she would return.

She momentarily panicked, feeling the darkness close in and she had the strange thought that this was where her claustrophobia came from, drowning in the blackness of a wide-open lake. But as she lost consciousness, she gained something else. She was descending down a hole much blacker than the water and she could no longer feel any cold or pain. When she finally stopped, it was not because she 'hit bottom'. There was no bottom here. Only blackness and a weird equilibrium that felt like she had stopped because this was simply where time began.

She slowly felt herself rising and around her there was only dark, she realized, because she had no body or eyes to perceive such a thing as light or color. As she reassembled herself, she felt as if she was a speck in the primordial volcanic blackness of time as it was first felt on earth. She rose higher and experienced a billion years in the blink of an eye. She realized that every living thing that ever evolved was hidden inside her being and she was remembering.

It was all happening so fast but she remembered that she was, at one point, a worm, a fish, a scorpion and any number of things before she became a woman. Not just any woman but the first one. The last one who remembered. After her, all others would forget but she wouldn't. She would remember her time as all things and she would be the mother of mankind. Until she wasn't…

She had another destiny. She opened her eyes to look up through water. She could see the light of the sun shining high above her as she escaped her death from drowning. Or did she? She felt as light as a feather, loosed from her bonds. The ties that had bound her to the depth were gone and she was rising so fast that she almost shot out of the water and skittered across the ice.

She could only see light, no images but had imagined her names with every moment of her ascent. Five thousand five hundred and fifty-five years, she had been at the bottom of the lake and she had promised to come back for her granddaughter. And so, she would keep her promise. A hand picked her up not long after she surfaced and she was plunged into the rough darkness of a bag.

She heard the voices. "This is a good one. Looks old. We don't see too many of these anymore."

As she started to lose cognition again, she tried to remember her name. Ah sat? Asatru? Au Set? Auses? Isis? Aisette? Asietta? she was going dark again and then, all she heard were the sounds…

Bells. From the front she could hear yelling, "Hello!? Anyone here?" It was the bell she put on the shop door that woke her.

"Oh my god!" She tried to reshape her hair as she rushed out into the front trying to calm her nerves and pretend everything was fine. "Oh, it's you…" She realized how that sounded as she saw Max at the door stomping the snow off his feet.

"I'm happy to see you too…"

She laughed. "I'm sorry, I spaced out for a few minutes there. But I'm glad you're here, I have to ask you something. Come look at my catalogue. I have to show you my new Isis…" She went into the back to grab her catalogue and she opened it to the page she had bookmarked and handed it to Max. "Isn't she beautiful?"

Max looked puzzled. "'Venus of Lausanne?' Looks like a lot of cash considering she's, literally, just 'flotsam and jetsam'."

Catherine grabbed the catalogue. It had opened to the wrong page. Instead of an Isis replica, it was the little jet 'Venus' that the old woman wore. It was not a replica and had been found on the shores of Lake Geneva in Lausanne Switzerland. She was about to tell Max it was a mistake but she knew it wasn't. This was her Isis. Her tastes were too expensive for her own store.

CHAPTER 14

They had agreed to meet on a Sunday afternoon when the shop was closed. She was actually surprised her husband let her go. She was expecting much more of a protest than what he gave her and then she remembered it was Superbowl Sunday.

The normal routine she went through whenever she wished to go out on her own involved, making arrangements for the kids, expecting him to not feel well prior to her leaving, having him come up with excuses for things in an attempt to guilt her into staying home, starting an argument that led him, preemptively, to accuse her of cheating, telling her no one would love her like he did and, if all else failed, he would hint at or outright threaten suicide. Because he owned a loaded gun, this terrified her.

She'd had a couple of readings before, they usually didn't last long and they never really told her much. In fact, she normally felt that she knew more about the reader by the time they were done than they could ever glean from her. So she figured she'd be home in an hour or two at the most. She would get dinner ready and make sure everything was running smoothly for the kids before they started in on their school week again the next day.

Three hours later, her reading with Theo was still going strong. Her cell phone rang, for the second time, interrupting them.

"What the hell is taking so long?" came the terse question from the other end.

"Um, well, it's still going on... I'm guessing maybe another half hour?" She looked at Theo for confirmation as she talked. He shrugged and said, "Maybe more like an hour or so."

"Okay, well closer to an hour. I will call you when I'm leaving."

She ended the conversation as quickly as she could but was feeling that sick, nervous feeling in her gut which always accompanied his anger and impatience. It was hard to focus on the information Theo was giving her as her thoughts were distracted by her fear of what she would face upon her return home.

As Theo spoke, she noticed a thin cord of leather around his neck. She thought of her own thin leather cord and wondered what Theo's held. With her eyes, she followed it down until it disappeared beneath his shirt but not before noticing the white color of a bone? A tooth? There was something attached to the end and mostly concealed by his collar.

"I'm sorry, I don't mean to interrupt but what is that?" She motioned to his necklace.

"This?" he pulled on the leather to reveal a wire wrapped claw.

"It's a bear claw."

Catherine immediately remembered her dream. She stared at it quietly for what must have been a little too long.

"Are you okay?"

"Why a bear claw?"

"Well, this one is a gift from my teacher who is called 'Mahto' or 'Bear', the People call me 'Mahtociqala' or 'little bear'." The way he said 'the people' made her feel as if he had been well loved and respected and as if he had whole lives lived in this one lifetime.

"Which People?"

He laughed. "These were Blackfoot and Oglala but the Candomble of Brazil call me Osito because my African Yoruba Teacher was also called 'Baba Theo' and they called him 'Oso' or 'Bear'. Like 'Teddy Bear'. Get it? So I was Osito or 'Tito Otito' to them as well. 'Little Bear' or Uncle Baby Bear. Not really a spiritual name. They assumed I was gay like my teacher and that was many years and pounds ago." He laughed, rubbing his cleanly shaven head, "and you have to remember I was a lot furrier back then"

She smiled and noticed his eyes. Sometimes she saw such light and joy, like she did now, when he laughed. Other times she noticed a magical, almost dangerous, darkness there. It wasn't something that made her afraid, however. Instead when she saw it, she noticed her body would react in a way that somewhat embarrassed her as her own internal darkness would stir in response.

Theo flipped over a card. He used a deck with Mayan symbology. She wasn't familiar with it so she couldn't "read ahead", in a sense, when he turned them. But this one triggered something in her. A picture of a man and a woman facing each other, their wrists were tied together and there seemed to be some stormy or celestial thing going on above their heads. She noticed the darkness that flicked past his eyes when he registered the image.

"Have you ever heard of a 'Teacher Tyrant'?"

"Not really."

"Sometimes we find ourselves with people who treat us badly, people who push us to the edge, who force us to see things differently. These people teach us the things that are vital for us to learn, or in your case, to remember."

Catherine remained quiet and thoughtful as he continued.

"All this going on above it, that's Great Spirit. Really, it's his mother, XochiQuetzal. It means there is a reason for all of this. You're being pushed to realize your Destiny. The one with a capital 'D'." This time he was the one thoughtful and quiet.

"The other way of looking at this card is to know it can represent two people who are brought together by Spirit, and by shared destinies, in a more positive way. They are bound together in a partnership that furthers their destiny that of the Great Spirit's."

"Which one is this?"

Theo looked at her and smiled, "You have to choose…"

He continued to turn cards and to talk. There was a lot of information and her eyes would sometimes glaze over and she wouldn't catch it all. She was still distracted by time and what awaited her at home. She hated that she had trouble focusing.

"Your reading is heavy on ancestral influence. I'll bet you've had some strange things happening to you lately. Sometimes when you begin to awaken to a lot of things at once it can feel a bit like you're going crazy. Some people actually do. Some can't accept the changes, or open their self to possibilities, too scared and stuck in old ways. Sometimes, they shut down, give up or revert. On occasion, they may even have a nervous breakdown or simply choose to live in a comfortable level of pain."

"That's not a particularly comforting thought"

He smiled but said nothing.

"Look, it's been pretty obvious from these cards that you've been living a double life."

Catherine laughed, deflecting a truth she already knew, "I'm hardly a spy." She tried to make a joke and distract from the seriousness she felt creeping up on her. She didn't like that he seemed about to discover who she was inside.

Here she was in a crazy shop, filled with all sorts of things that made people nervous. She didn't belong to any covens or women's groups. She had no one telling her what to do. She hadn't had any help on this adventure so far. She had all sorts of crazy intuitions and dreams. She was being driven to follow them, almost obsessed, and she didn't even know why.

She could have pretended, she could have stayed as this perfect wife and mother, living in suburbia, going to soccer games on Saturdays and Catholic Church on Sundays. She could just smile sweetly, knowing which fork to use at luncheons and how to speak 'Republican' at D.A.R. functions. Except she couldn't.

She could feel that darkness in her rising up so strongly. Or maybe it wasn't rising. Maybe she was. Or was she drowning? She grasped the little jet figurine under her sweater. She suddenly felt that it wanted to yell out at injustices, howl at the moon, make magic potions, dance naked outside, talk with the crows and scare away all the people that annoyed her.

Or maybe she was just projecting on a little piece of overpriced burnt petrified wood. Maybe those were just her own wishes. She thought about showing Theo her 'Isis' but it would be too hard to explain. She sensed that whatever it was, it would scare people. Theo might not be scared but she did not want to risk it. Her Isis had come to her in such an odd and dark way that it was a little too real. Too spooky.

She usually liked the idea of scaring people. It sounded much more fun than to always be the one who was scared. And she was scared. What if she let that part of her escape? What if people knew who she really was? If she could only let a bit of it out, a sort of compromise, why couldn't that work? Why couldn't she just hint at things, but laugh them off or justify them if someone were to call her our or question her?

She didn't want to be questioned. She hated conflict. She hated disappointing people when they discovered she wasn't who they thought she was. She felt bad and as if she were somehow wrong for believing what she did, for seeing the world as she did, for listening to the voices, for feeling the spirits around her, for following her instincts. It all seemed so normal to her but she was reminded time and time again that it wasn't. She began to fear the darkness less and was instead terrified of the light.

"You won't be able to fake it forever." Theo said quietly as if he had heard this whole inner dialogue. "These things you are being pushed to do, to discover, to understand will change you. Now that you've begun, you can't go back."

She worked hard to hold back the tears. She wasn't going to let him see that she was afraid. She could be brave for her kids, she could be brave when it came to business, but she was terrified of revealing her own heart.

As Theo spoke, he realized that as much information as he was getting, there was more to the story than he was allowed to see. The only time this would happen to him is when he was to be part of that story. He wondered how he fit in her's?

Following the reading, Catherine felt almost as if a long-locked door in her had been cracked open. She was tempted to shut it again, but as he already seemed to know, she felt less inclined to hide. Maybe if she didn't hide, this one time, she would have someone to talk to and they could become really good friends.

Over the next weeks and months, he proved himself to be just that. Which was strange to her as she made sure never to count any men among her friends. Obviously, male friends would cause great difficulty in her marriage. In addition, it always seemed inevitable that her so called friend would, at some point in time, make a move on her.

Strangely though, she didn't feel this pressure from Theo. He was so polite. In all the conversations they had that day and after, never once did he even hint at anything inappropriate. She began to wonder if maybe he really was gay? She had been so conditioned, she even questioned her attractiveness.

Theo would often give her hugs and a quick platonic kiss goodbye whenever he left the shop, at times, even in front of her husband. Which made her extremely nervous. But he was so casual about it. And she simply told her husband, "It's a California thing." knowing it would play right into his stereotypes and take the pressure off of her. But the arguments at home, however, were increasing. The accusations were constant. The threats were becoming more physical.

When she arrived home following the reading, her husband decided to 'punish' her lateness by yelling, threatening, then finally storming out. Theo had been right, it was time for her to choose… She realized as he drove off for the hundredth time that any ties that had bound them were no longer there.

ABSINTHE, ALEWIVES & ALCHEMY

CHAPTER 15

The woman held the reins of the little wagon loosely. The horses knew to follow the lead wagon and she was only there if they needed to stop. They did the rest. The beautiful white horses were the real heart of the little traveling show and she was just filler between their stunning performances.

The breed had come up with her people from India and were really bred for the military but when her part of the kingdom revolted it sent her people into Africa and Spain and, eventually to Sicily. Now they were moving again. The Romans had declared the Sindhi as heretics and so they were going to go to France or the Swiss Cantons where they might be free.

They had been a Carnivale troupe but that was now forbidden so they had become a 'Commedia dell'Arte' troupe, telling the traditional Roman tales. But people really came to see the horses and the acrobats and anyone who knew the Roma Circuses also knew that, after the shows in the day, they might find other, more earthly delights and amusements with these people at night.

The woman holding the reins was born in this wagon. She had heard that her father had made it as a gift for her mother but she did not know him nor what had become of him. And while the symbols and paintings of 'The Lovers' were a part of the traditional story, it was also a sign to those who knew that the woman inside was for hire as a 'lover' as well. The woman at the reins knew this as her fate as it had been her mother's before her. Her mother was too old now and so she became the 'Tasseomancera' or Tea Leaf Reader on a wagon painted with the Fatta Morae or 'The Fates'.

The wagon with the Braggadocio or 'braggart' soldiers was the Strongman who owned the circus and also owned she and her mother. He wrestled a bear for the crowd and fought anyone willing to put up a wager. She would collect the money for the wagers and entice men into fighting to save her honor. They would wager to win her from him. She collected a lot of money over her years but no one ever won that bet. At night he would rent her out to those too cowardly to win her outright by fighting him.

Her mother too, had endured this fate and, when her daughter was pretty enough, she gave her up to the same after a particularly vicious beating had left her with a horribly broken nose. Her mother had tried to quit and take her daughter away when she noticed his attentions were turning to her. She knew this day would come. Not because she had divined it but because that was the way things were.

Her daughter was not as accepting. She knew she was too young and pretty to be beaten so she did what she could to enrage the strongman they called Saathi, as a way to get back at him, knowing that to beat her would make her 'unrentable'. Saathi's whole Hindu name meant 'babble like a brook' for the way he never seemed to stop talking but they had told him, instead, that it meant 'Master'. He had come from a rich 'Gadjo' Roman family but, she had heard, he had had to leave town for killing a man. Her mother wouldn't talk about it.

He had claimed that he had bought the circus from a Roma and owned all of the performers as well. He had paid more for the horses than the four performers but Roma people could not travel as free persons and he was a Free Roman who owned them now. He pretended to be Oublier, partially for money but also because he was wanted for more than one murder. They had had to leave too quickly in more than one town for fights that had gone too far or because the Strongman resorted to poisoning to make sure that he never lost his standing wager.

Rome had begun to crack down on the Roma, so he had decided to go to France or Geneva where he could be free to ply his 'trade' without the Church's interference. They would try to go to Rome before Easter to make as much money as they could during the Festiva Rites, then they would leave during Lent and aim to be in France by Easter.

The two horseman he also owned were getting on in years and he hoped to buy a new trainer from one of the other circuses that performed on the roads to the Holy City for pilgrims. If he made enough money, he thought he would also like to buy another girl. A younger one. The Sindhi snake charmer turned out to be a useful ally that he had purchased soon after leaving Sicily, so he would keep him, as long as he kept him informed and the others in line.

In the days leading up to the Pilgrim Roads, the young girl who was called 'Eva' in the morality play show during the day was renamed 'Lilita' after dark to entice the men willing to pay for a fallen beauty. But as she held loosely on the reins, she tried to remember the last time she had been called by her real name of 'Sarita'. She had been named for Durga Kali as a baby before she and her mother were captured and enslaved in Sicily when she was a small child. Her mother, she was told, had been a real circus performer before being forced to join this one.

Sarita was thinking of names because she was wondering what to call her own daughter and was counting how many days until she would show. She thought that she might make it to Lent but she was already feeling sick. Her mother knew and had offered to 'make it better' with a tea of Wormwood and Rue but something inside her made her want to keep this baby despite the possibility of who the probable father was.

It was a possibility but she also clearly remembered the night she had given him the 'Maloich' or evil eye and he had not touched her since. She thought of that night and counted back the days since she had used her 'fascinum', the little black charm that she had placed in a silver locket and made him fear her gaze. She did not know where she had learned it. It seemed to be something she just 'remembered'.

She felt him come up behind her one day. She turned deliberately, slowly to face him. It was as if Kali or a thousand grandmothers were staring back at him through her eyes. Whatever it was, she looked at him as words came out of her mouth unbidden. She hissed, 'Om Krim Kali, Kali Ma!' Perhaps they had come from her new daughter growing inside her and it was she who had 'the gift'.

Sarita's mother also had 'the gift'. As the wagons slowed into a clearing she pulled alongside her mother's wagon and her mother looked at her. She knew everything. She not only read the leaves but she was an Asietta, a diviner and oracle. Something she hid from their owner but not a thing she would be able to hide for much longer.

"You have decided to keep her, haven't you?" It was not a question. "You know he will kill us both. I have seen it."

"I know it and know why you put our show horses to my wagon."

They watched as Saathi unhitched his work horses from the lead wagon and let them go out to graze. As he uncoupled the bear's wagon from his own, he stopped to share a drink with the snake charmer. He liked to keep the bear hungry so it would menace the crowds and eat and drink in front of the beast to taunt it. The two older horsemen pulled alongside on their horses, dismounted and bowed low to their master.

It took less than a minute to happen. Saathi doubled over like he was in sudden pain and the snake charmer hit his bald head with a hammer used to stake the tents. The horsemen took him down and brandishing the tent mallets, they killed their owner tormentor. The snake charmer looked back and saw the women transfixed by what was happening. "Do not watch, Go! Run. Go to Motta, Madame. The Dominicans will give you Sanctuary!"

Sarita whipped the reins but could not help glancing back to see his body being dragged into the Bear wagon. She did not have to see more.

Sarita's mother took the reins and the beautiful white horses ran as if they knew what had just occurred. They ran for nearly six leagues and it was dark before they finally stopped.

Sarita had been silent as they had driven, taking turns holding the reins. Her mother had already stolen the big man's money as well as his great scimitar. The others were, by now, burying what was left of his body.

"How did you know that Sanjay would not betray us?" She did not trust the snake charmer.

Kalimaa, her mother, almost said, "because Saathi, the Babbling One, killed Sanjay's father." Instead, she told her daughter, "It is Vendetta." She got down to let the horses feed. "He will not tell. He can keep a secret."

Sarita shook her head. He sure could! She had no idea and she thought herself intuitive. "But… How did you know?"

"Sanjay is your brother."

Sarita stared at her mother open mouthed. Her mother smiled. "They did not name me Kalimaa because I am a great beauty." She led the horses to a nearby stream and Sarita followed with too many questions and nowhere to start. "We have a long way to the Alps. I will tell you then. For now, we are just pilgrims going to Geneva to join the rest of our circus for Carnavale."

In a month, they had found the monastery in the hills above Geneva and took Sanctuary with the escaped Cistercian heretics who had joined the Dominican nuns who had also escaped Benedictine persecution in a free Switzerland. They were welcomed because Kalimaa had recognized the black Madonna being transported on a road out of Geneva and bowed low to her as she passed by.

The monks merely nodded and would have continued but when the woman that they had taken for prostitutes by their cart and dress, spoke the words clearly, touching her heart, they suddenly stopped.

"Terra Stella." She said, and both she and daughter, curtsied low.

"Terra Stella, quaeso boni Fratres." Said the daughter in perfect Latin. That meant many things but up in the hills outside of town, it was a plea for sanctuary. The brothers turned their wagon around and led the two women to safety in the hills.

Many months later, Kalimaa Madhu became Sr. Mary Aisetta and took her vows on the day that her granddaughter was born. Since she was not married, she took the name of the place where she was born and became Ana Aisette Mari Louise De la Motta d'Dea.

An unmarried mother could not stay at the monastery so she took the wagon to a town called Couvet. A place where she heard that there was a circus full of Romas and Sindhis, whom the Swiss called Jennischers, just outside of that town in the Val.

There, she made her home until the plagues came again and she knew that she must return to the fort where her mother had recently died to take up her place making the Absinthe. Once again, she loaded up the little wagon, the one that her father had so lovingly made for her mother all those years ago. She looked at her daughter, now a teenager, and hoped that, one day, she would have a lover like the ones painted on its walls.

For her, given her history with all men, the only lover she would have was as a 'Bride of Christ', like her mother, who had recently passed, was before her.

ABSINTHE, ALEWIVES & ALCHEMY

CHAPTER 16

After her reading, Catherine had a better understanding of the conflicts with her husband. She was no longer the woman he married or even who he knew last year. He saw it as if he were losing her but the truth was, he had never had her. His behavior, in that new light, made sense to Catherine but did little to excuse it.

She also realized that she probably would have put up with it for her whole life but her pretending would not, could not create a better life for her daughters. She knew he would get worse as she became more and more the woman she always had been.

She would constantly work to diffuse situations that could lead to outbursts. She had all sorts of strategies. One she resorted to on a particularly stressful evening was to make him his favorite dinner, creamed tuna on toast. It was one of his favorites that she thought was disgusting and it reminded her of the chipped beef recipe they used to call 'shit on a shingle'. It was the same idea, only made with tuna instead.

She had just begun stirring the flour into the butter over the stove top when he came into the kitchen, looked over her shoulder and into the saucepan. He sometimes fancied himself Chef Gordon

Ramsay even though he couldn't cook like him or cook at all. But he could scream like him, "I thought I told you NO LUMPS! You can't make it like that, there will be *LUMPS*. I TOLD YOU *NO LUMPS!*". He proceeded to grab the pan off of the burner and throw it across the kitchen into the sink. "God damn it! You can't do anything right!" He stormed from the kitchen to the garage, slamming the door behind him so hard that the glass shattered.

Catherine took a deep breath, swept up the glass, cleaned out the pan that was thrown, then made 'PB&J' sandwiches and popcorn for dinner. She and the girls ate quietly in the living room. Thankfully, He didn't come back home until after everyone had gone to bed.

She made sure to pretend she was asleep when he finally entered their bedroom but it didn't work. Damn. He wanted sex. The last thing in the world she wanted to even think about at that point. She was feeling sick with anxiety and sadness, hardly a good precursor to sex. Telling him that, however, was the wrong thing.

He moved himself on top of her and screamed through gritted teeth, "What the hell is wrong with you?" He cried, "You never want it when I do." Then, a paranoid pause. "...Cause you're getting it somewhere else? Aren't you?" He slammed both his fists repeatedly down on the mattress inches away from either side of her. "Aren't you?" he repeated as he rolled off her and slammed his fists against the dresser, breaking a drawer. She lay there perfectly still and worked to calm her breathing.

He looked at the broken drawer and got quiet. He started to cry. "I'm so sorry." he said as he climbed back into bed. "I'm so sorry. I promise, I won't do it again." She'd heard it time and again and said nothing in response. He rolled over to her, touching her, pressing up against her. "I know, I'm a loser, worthless. I don't know why you love me." he slipped a hand up under her shirt and she stiffened, froze. He sobbed, "I just can't take it anymore".

He rolled her over pressed his body on hers, pinning her and taking what he wanted. She closed her eyes and let him, all the while praying for it to be over quickly. When it was, she turned away and let silent tears fall into the darkness.

As he drifted to sleep, he reached out and placed his hand on her back. His touch triggered such a disgust, a revulsion she had never known and she had to swallow back the vomit that rose in her throat and she knew it was more than from just this lifetime.

The next morning, she couldn't bring herself to look him in the eye. It was as if something in her had finally snapped. It wasn't the first time he had forcibly insisted on sex. But she knew that, somehow, she had to make this time the last.

A steely coldness crept into her. She could feel a powerful darkness rise up from her groin and into her heart. She felt it squeeze the air from her lungs and when it reached her throat, it pushed out her breath carrying with it, the whispered, almost guttural words, 'Om Krim Kali, Kali Ma'. Her fear was now replaced by some sort of ancient anger, the words had come unknown and unbidden from somewhere deep inside and long ago.

It had engulfed her completely by the time he came into the kitchen where she stood stirring eggs for breakfast. She only glanced at him as he reached out to grab her and lean in for a kiss. But that was enough. The look in her eyes repelled him as if he had been physically pushed. Something there that triggered his own distant, dangerous memory.

The house was tense and silent after that and, luckily, two days later, he left town for a business trip and would be gone for four days. It was instantly happier and lighter at home. There was laughter and play. Marie said she wished her dad would never come back, "I like it when he's gone. He just ruins it". On one hand, Catherine completely understood her daughter's feelings and, at the same time, it broke her heart.

She remembered the first day she met her husband. She had been working in an office and he was waiting outside in a lobby. As she was filing some paperwork, she had the eerie feeling that she was being watched. She looked up and right into his eyes as they watched her from across the room.

She instantly felt uneasy. A feeling of strange recognition accompanied the warning in her gut screaming at her. Still, she dismissed it. The reaction was so sudden and unexpected that she rationalized that it was unreasonable, illogical and hardly fair. So, later, when he asked her out, she accepted.

Why the hell had she not listened to her instinct? It wasn't just one date. Why was she always denying her intuition, her innate abilities? Then she looked at her girls, she was so thankful for them. There were always reasons, she had to believe that. Had to.

And now she believed it was over. *Knew* it was over. Now, she was just hoping to buy herself a little more time to make a plan of action, to figure out exactly how to leave. Safely.

Her girls stayed with her late at the shop that night because Max was holding his 'Wicca 101' workshop and her husband was still out of town. She and Max had become good friends. He would complain about his boyfriend and she would complain about her husband. They would talk art and history. He knew so much about magic and though he was teaching basics through Wicca, he was really developing his own religion. Or, really, a non-religion. Like her, he would listen to his spirits, his dreams and his intuitions and he allowed himself to be guided by his heart. He was a good teacher and, also, a good friend.

There were about eight people in attendance that night. She had been getting to know them through this class. She was really having fun with it all. It was a great escape but it had been causing untold strife at home. Then, she thought, 'What didn't?'

This was the last class; the atmosphere was light. When the phone rang it startled her more than it should have. "Where are you?" he asked without saying hello.

"I'm at the shop. It's Tuesday, remember? It's a workshop night."

"Where are the girls?"

"They're with me, I wouldn't leave them home alone."

"They shouldn't be around that witch stuff. It's Satanism"

She sighed, "No. No, it's not at all Satanism. That's something else entirely, we've been through this." She sighed.

He began to scream again, about anything and everything. She walked to the back room and tried to be calm. Her anger and anxiety were rising. Her body was shaking from too much adrenaline but it was much more than just that...

He was yelling now so loudly, she was sure they heard in the other room. "I can't take this anymore! I can't keep going on like this!" He was increasingly ranting and irrational. Then in the heat of his screaming rage he yells through the phone, "What do you want? Do you want a divorce?" Then. Silence.

Time seemed to slow just then. The voice she heard seemed to come from far away and not from within her at all. "Yes." was the quiet answer. It was her own voice... "Yes, I do."

And that was that. There was no going back. She had not said it before. She had never threatened it. She had promised herself a long time ago that she would not stoop to bullying tactics in the heat of an argument or any time else. When the words came out, she knew it was the most honest thing she had ever said. So did he.

The tears that followed wracked her body. It all seemed to happen so fast then. She couldn't hide any of this from anyone. She was glad Max was there, she wished her daughters weren't. The pain she felt when she told her girls what had happened was physical.

She was embarrassed that this was happening in front of the people at the workshop. But they weren't the type of people who would judge. Their support, too, was immeasurable. This was not how she had imagined her life. This was never what she had wanted. But like Isis and Inanna before her, she had begun her descent. There was no turning back now.

The days and weeks that followed were surreal. She and her husband were still living together while they hammered out the details of the separation. She tried to avoid him as much as possible. Both of them stayed away when they could. He would sometimes come home after obviously having had too much to drink and would scream and threaten her. Her children were having nightmares and had a hard time sleeping alone.

Her youngest had climbed into bed with her one night. She would make up stories to tell her to keep her mind off of things and help her to go to sleep. But he came home before she had drifted off and proceeded to pound loudly on the locked bedroom door. He pleaded with her to come out and talk with him. Then he demanded. She told him to be quiet, explaining that the girls were sleeping and that they would talk in the morning.

But he continued to try the locked door handle, he shook it and pounded some more. He threatened to smash her goddesses on the mantle, to destroy the house. He threatened anything he could think of that he thought would get her to leave the locked room. Her "things" meant nothing compared to her children and safety.

Her daughter shook in her arms as she tried her best to soothe her, all the while listening for her oldest who was upstairs by herself in her room. She prayed to her ancestors, to the goddess, to anyone who may listen to keep her daughter safe, to keep him from going upstairs. She tried to make a plan of what she would do if he decided to go upstairs after her. Fear for herself was nothing compared to the fear for her children. She would do anything to keep them safe. Eventually, he passed out on the sofa and night fell into an uneasy quiet disrupted only by the incessant pounding of her heart. But at least it wasn't the door.

The next evening, he came home again, alcohol on his breath and a temper in his soul. He began screaming at her as she stood in the living room. Her daughters had gone upstairs to get ready for bed. She willed them to stay there and to stay quiet.

He stepped threateningly towards her. She demanded that he leave.

"You're out of control. You can't be here right now. Go!" She did her best to sound strong though she felt nothing of the sort.

"You think you can make me leave? This is MY house, bitch!"

The screaming went on but she didn't really remember what he was saying, everything seemed distant and surreal. She could vaguely hear herself yelling, "Get out! Get out! Get out!" over and over again while trying not to cry.

It was then that she saw him, plain as day. He was standing to her right, between her and her husband. It was Theo. It startled her, confused her, but it also gave her comfort. She felt stronger and somehow safer. She knew he wasn't be real, but he looked so real.

Though he wasn't really tall, he seemed to be rising up, almost like a bear. Why would *he* be here? Why would *he* show up? So many mixed emotions, questions, confusion, everything at once. Her husband didn't seem to see or react to him. Theo was not even acknowledging him. He was just holding his pipe, looking at her and his gaze held her. Catherine did not know if he could be felt or if it was her own fearless gaze staring past him that made her husband feel suddenly insignificant and impotent. Either way, her husband suddenly decided to leave and Catherine collapsed on the floor and cried.

CHAPTER 17

The months that followed her decision to divorce were partly a blur of emotion and numbness but at the same time, they were a relief. The dreams came with increasing frequency and they seemed to be all telling a story. Lifetimes, all hers, seemed to be hurtling towards a single lifetime and they all seemed to be working 'this', her waking lifetime.

She also noticed that she had more 'knowings'. Not information as much as the unsettling feeling that a thing that had not been in her awareness, now, suddenly, was. Often it was after one of her 'head tingles' on what she now knew was her 'crown chakra'. Sometimes, she would be talking to someone and stuff would just come pouring out of her mouth before she knew or could stop it.

This was true of her dreams as well. For instance, she knew that the mother of the priest was eventually killed by the Romans when she returned to become the queen bee of all of the hives. Each of the hives had what they called their own 'trade', a word that felt more like 'alchemy' than 'barter'.

She had always read that alchemy was old learned men trying to turn lead into gold. The truth was that the real magic was the trade of turning grapes into wine, barley into beer, wheat into bread, the sick into the healthy and, even, the living to the dead. Then, she had read Paracelsus 'Many have said of Alchemy, that it is for the making of gold and silver. For me such is not the aim, but to consider only what virtue and power may lie in medicines.' Written by the man who had stolen so much from women who would be accused of witchcraft while he would go on to be the 'Father of Modern Medicine'.

She mentioned these knowings to Max during one of their conversations. "That makes sense." he said. "The Greeks thought of extracting metals but the word really means to get the sap or juice out of something. They stole the word from the Egyptians but then they got obsessed with the whole gold thing."

The mother in her dream had returned after Vanos' son had grown up to become a scholar like his fathers. Although she had made a name and small fortune in Couvet, she had, once again, donned the rough robes of the 'Alewives' and returned to the monastery.

There she made her vats of fresh ale in the winter and bier in the summer when hops were available. It was this same mother in her dream who was showing her that making dinner was not that much different than making medicines, getting gold not as important as transmuting or saving the essence or the juice of a thing. Not to women whose survival and alchemy required no gold.

The modern Catherine realized that working with yeasts, fungi and bacteria must have seemed magical, at least to the women who had found a way to create and prolong perishable food as well as to create their own economy, sustainability and freedom.

She already knew from her experiments with tea that killing the 'gall' on one of her herbs with pesticides removed the curative powers of that herb and so organic herbs were important to her.

Max had told her that another word for alchemy was 'chemia' that the Greeks took to mean 'metals' but it really meant 'black earth' or living soil. "They were transmuting poop and not gold. Alchemy is the real shit!" he laughed. She rolled her eyes.

Max had an encyclopedic knowledge of 'the crafts' and she was learning from him that words like 'Pagan', 'Heathen' and 'Witch' weren't religions or cultures but rather names that were given by the Church in order to take away someone's culture, property or even life. She treasured their talks for his knowledge but also his friendship as she began to see her own life in light of all of these things were a part of her new 'adult sized reality' as Max called it.

Their conversations triggered memories. From her dreams for sure but also from parts of those times that she did not see. Like she had a sudden realization that each of the 'hives' were hiding their 'craft'. Not 'witchcraft' but their culture and things they brought with them from the countries they had escaped from.

One night as she lay awake, she saw herself as a Polish Jewish woman sorting 'bog ore' in the rich soils above Lake Geneva that would be made into weapons of the finest steel. She watched as her own hands sifted and sorted thousands of tiny beads of ore from loads of dirt that she used in 'Her' monastery garden. Alchemy.

Her hands were black from the iron and rich dirt that was harvested from bogs nearby that were just like the Peat bogs of their original home 500 miles to the north in Poland. This was the same monastery where the son was burned alive and upside down in the aftermath of one of Cat's dreams and also where 'Juden', Jewish, iron was being smelted. It was this trade, this 'craft', perfected by Polish 'Juden' who knew the secret of bog ore that first drew the attention of the Romans who demanded to know the secret of the fine, hard steel used for making superior swords.

This wasn't the only 'witchcraft' they were all accused of. They made ale that wouldn't 'turn'. Bier was originally of the devil. They made Absinthe. They refused to tell the church because 'Wormwood and Gall' was a sin in the Bible. They simply refused to respond to the makeshift inquisition. This was not an acceptable answer and the women of all six 'hives' were killed by having their head crushed on the cubit stone she had first seen as the little boy.

The Romans killed the women in order to steal their crafts but failed to realize that killing them as 'witches' also meant that their secrets died with them. No woman gave in to the Romans even as they were killed one by one. Often it was because they simply did not see what they were doing as evil, magic or alchemy.

The visions were really upsetting to Catherine and she knew that had the women been allowed to live they would have uncovered the secret of how bog iron and gold nuggets were made. Instead, they were killed and their knowledge with them.

Alchemy, she realized, was also 'witchcraft' and the alchemy of everyday things was more valuable than gold itself. She couldn't stop thinking of all the women dying just for passing on the ways of their mothers and grandmothers. Alchemy was only witchcraft if a woman was the one doing it.

In her mind, she understood this but couldn't get past their deaths almost as if they were her own. It was like she wasn't dreaming as much as they were talking to her, telling her their stories as soon as she lay down or rested.

It was Jennische Sinti peoples that brought beer and Greeks kefir of the Aethanikos 'heath dwellers', the 'ethnics', or what we call 'Heathens', that saved the populations during the plague with Absinthe. Her Oublier ancestors were wandering chemists turned alchemists. Her 'Paganis' ancestors were physicians called metaphysicians and her Celtic forebears were bringing such 'witchery' as making wool or even the healing cheeses that came from nearby Neuchatel.

Theo listened as she told him her latest dreams. "Sounds like 'burning times' memories." He added, "It's a thing."

He explained this 'thing' as something that was happening worldwide. Women having dreams, memories, sudden knowings of things that had happened at other times. Hidden or forgotten things. He said, "I bet you thought you're going crazy. Don't worry." He paused and winked, "You are…"

This weirdly made her feel better, especially since she had never liked 'religions' or 'cults'. She began to realize that her tea blending was her witchcraft, as was her sourdough bread. The cheeses and kombucha her friends made was theirs. Even the Tirggel cookies she made had spices used to cure the plague and brand women in Switzerland and Italy as witches. Max listened to her newfound 'memory' and added, "Don't forget wine…" then he added, "I don't want to sound like I don't believe in higher magic. How else would all of this have been discovered?"

Later that night, she sat up in her favorite chair after the girls had gone to bed. It was big enough to curl up in and she was not surprised that she had fallen asleep. When she opened her eyes again, she was no longer in her living room. Instead, she was the priest, who was the little boy, who was really a girl, who was her ancestor. The one that was burned upside down. But why?

She entered that dream to see that the world was upside down. Her hair was unbound and hanging, entangled in branches of kindling. A Roman Centurion flanked by Roman priests were directly in front of her and the Roman read from a scroll of parchment.

"You are accused of the heresy of witchcraft and the productions of Idols disguised as the Mother of Our Lord. How do you plead?"

She heard the words come out of her mouth, slowly as if in pain. She was. As if she had been whipped. She had been. And as if she had not had food or drink for three days and nights. She had not.

"I am guilty only of showing the world that Mari is Eisatt and the Love of God."

The priests listened and stepped back to confer. 'Eisatt' was a recognized name for the Mother Mary but in light of the fact that he had chosen to make her black, he was obviously naming 'The Love of God' as 'Eisatt' or 'Isis'. An Abomination.

The Roman priests each whispered to the Roman soldier who rolled up the scroll. "Scribe, enter it into the record that the priest uttered abominations to God and refused to admit his heresy.

Also, note that, when hung upside down it was discovered that the priest is actually a woman in the guise of a man. Another abomination. Finally, the image of 'Our Lady' as an 'Egyptienne Isis' or Aisata is the final and fatal abomination and he will be put to death by fire at the sealing of this verdict."

With this, he stabbed the pointed tip of a sharp knife into her neck and allowed drops of blood to fall on the verdict parchment. A wax seal was dripped on to it by one priest and the other, pressed his ring into the melted wax. All three crossed themselves and Catherine suddenly realized that her arms were free and she crossed herself in unison with the others.

This was only temporary, though, as each priest grabbed a hand and the soldier nailed her wrists to the X shaped posts with long thin iron spikes. The blood draining out of her caused a brief moment of hyper clarity but the smell of her own hair on fire was to be her last memory. A memory of a burning time.

CHAPTER 18

"Damn it, damn it, damn it" she whispered as she woke. Already covered in sweat, over-adrenalized and shaking, she felt her life to be a mess. These dreams were not helping. Mumbling to herself as she realized she had fallen asleep in the living room, "Crap, what time is it?" she said to herself as she fumbled for her phone to check the clock on the glowing screen. "3 am. 'The Witching Hour'. How appropriate".

Sitting up in the big chair, she considered her options, go to bed and catch a couple of more hours of sleep? Or maybe give up on the idea of rest, start the coffee early and try to figure out why she felt like she had been getting such heavy downloads of… what? Information? Identity? Insanity? What the hell was she supposed to do with all of this anyway?

It seemed that ever since her heart had been cracked open, so had her spirit, her intuition and now her mind. The first person she thought about talking to was Theo. He'd been through a lot in his life, maybe he'd have some advice, even if he didn't, she somehow felt better being able to express all the things on her mind and in her heart to someone who seemed to understand.

She settled on tea as opposed to coffee. It made her feel closer to her Grandma. Her Grandmother would always make her a steaming cup, along with a piece of burnt toast topped with butter and cinnamon, cut into vertical strips.

Whether it was the charcoal burnt bread or the love with which it was made, it always made her feel better. She started to dip the tea bag and, instead, tore it open and poured the tea right into the water. She sipped the liquid memories and stared into the darkness of the tea and, then, the backyard.

She wished she could jump ahead to the future, to a better place. She was sure there must be something better she was headed for. But god it was crappy, this journey to wherever that was.

So many questions went through her mind. So many frustrations bubbled up. Every time she turned around there seemed to be another battle to fight, another attack from yet another angle.

Her 'soon to be ex' had finally moved out of the house and into an apartment. But that didn't stop him from sending her ten to twenty threatening emails a day, not to mention the constant phone calls she did her best to ignore. He had someone parked outside, watching the house at night. And there were times she could swear she was being followed.

She moved her kids back to the public school as they were being harassed following letters their father had sent to the Catholic school staff, accusing their mother of being a witch. "How very 16th century of him", she thought but was surprised at the reaction of the people there, buying into his lies. He would talk to whomever would listen, making her into a whore and a devil worshipper.

He would explain how he had to save his children from her and her Satanic ways. Every time she heard about another person believing him and distancing themselves from her, she felt incredulous, exhausted and sad. Especially since her dream of owning her store was being used as proof of her heresy.

Her most recent blow had been from her own divorce attorney who told her not to fight him in court because, she said, "The fact is Catherine, he presents better than you."

"Not much has changed from those burning times, has it?" She asked Theo one day as she was recounting her woes.

Theo smiled. "Nah, these aren't burning times…" He paused as she waited. "This is just your 'Dark Night of the Soul'."

Great. How was that better? There was not a thing she could do. the cold fact was, she was going to lose her home but she would keep her children. He played the custody card and knew she would do anything not to lose her children, nothing else mattered, nothing.

Theo was right though. This was not a burning time. She would survive and all of this was just squeezing the juice out of her, making her stronger, last longer. This was not like death but more like leavening. Life. She was being enlivened by unknown things and she would be changed but she would not die. Like Max said to her, "No time for a dirt nap just yet. You have shit to do." 'Shit-to-do' was Max's word for Destiny.

Though she had no idea where she was going to live, it didn't matter as long as she had her children. She soothed herself with the thought that she still had her business and her loan from the bank that kept her afloat during this economic downturn that was killing all her neighboring businesses. Until she didn't.

She called the bank one day after she had been refused to withdraw some funds. An awkwardly apologetic manager came on the line to tell her, in a stuttering manner, that her loan had been closed and she was unable to take any more credit out on it.

It seems that her ex had called in, cancelled it and that was that. She was not notified, not consulted. It didn't matter that her name was on it, it didn't matter that this was awarded to her as part of the financial settlement in the divorce or that she could prove it. Nothing seemed to matter but what *he* wanted.

Before she put her empty tea cup down, she stopped to swirl it before glancing at the tea leaves. She didn't like what she saw and chucked the leaves in the sink. She checked the clock. It was Friday, she'd have to wake the girls soon. She was bracing herself for the emotional drama and trauma that would ensue as soon as they remembered that it was 'his' weekend.

Just as Catherine's new friends were inspiring her to be brave and live her life in a way true to herself, she was inspiring her daughters to explore and express who they truly were. It did not go unnoticed by their father.

It went against every fiber of her being to make them go and she entertained the idea of running away with them on more than one occasion. But she had already been threatened by the courts as to what would happen if she didn't keep the visitation schedule.

She was getting into the habit of looking forward to going into her shop every day. It would be a distraction at least. She was adding evening hours to make more money and to keep busy. She would try not to think about how she would keep the shop going, about how she would have to find a second job, about how she was having no luck in finding affordable housing and that her daughters would probably once again have to change schools. On top of everything else, she also worried about their safety.

She returned to her shop after taking her girls to school. She went into the back with a little shiver, she couldn't think about all of that right now. She wished she didn't have to think about it ever. She grabbed the mail, only bills. Maybe, for a few hours, she could pretend. She put on her game face and walked back into the front of the store.

There was a small event that evening at her shop in honor of "Bad Poetry Day". It seemed that was a 'real thing', on the calendar anyway. It sounded like something fun and light to celebrate, something she really needed right now. There ended up being several people in attendance. Theo was one of them who joined.

He stopped in early and she had a chance to talk with him. She was feeling somewhat calmer by the time the shop closed and the event started. She felt no pressure about writing a poem, after all it was *supposed* to be bad. At least hers was. Everyone else seemed to have really put in the effort and there was some good stuff there. She loved how each was a distinct reflection of the person she had come to know, as well.

If nothing else, opening this shop had allowed her to finally meet some people that were much more like she was. Their creativity and openness were giving her the courage to express more of who she truly was and to test out who she was becoming.

When the party wrapped up, Theo stayed behind to help her clean. After the floors were swept and the safe locked up, she walked him to the back entrance. He leaned in to give her his customary quick kiss goodbye when something else inside her took hold. Instead of letting him go at that, she answered his kiss with one of her own, one she was not expecting.

She lingered on his lips, letting his tongue find hers, letting his hands press gently on her lower back. It felt almost as if time had stopped yet it was over in only seconds. When she pulled back, he smiled, they said their goodbyes and she closed the door.

Then, she started to shake again. She could feel so clearly the heat of his hands on her back, still, long after they were gone. She felt embarrassed and confused. Why did she just do that? It was as if her body had disabled her brain momentarily and it took over all the 'thinking' instead.

Now that her brain was back 'on line', it was racing to understand. Something had shifted. Something had happened. This was way more than a kiss. She could barely sleep that night and called him on the phone first thing when she got to the shop.

"Hi, it's Cat" she said, momentarily surprised she used the nickname she hadn't used in years. "I was hoping you could stop by today. I'd really like to talk with you." Her stomach was full of butterflies, really amazingly large butterflies. This was so unlike her. She had always thought of Theo as 'just a friend' and he was her friend, but was there something more? Now she was thinking of him in a wholly new light. Well, this was awkward. This was really bad timing. She couldn't trust anything in her life. Especially not this.

She decided she needed to talk with him, apologize and tell him she meant nothing by it, he needed to forget her transgression, forget this whole thing had happened. It was as if someone else had possessed her body that night, she wasn't in her right mind. Her right mind flashed to another lifetime, another store and, seemingly, someone else's mind.

But that was exactly it, she realized. She wasn't in her mind. Her body was doing the thinking, and the 'talking' and her body never lied to her. Oh, her mind was a master of rationalizing, justifying, twisting and surviving. Her body though, had no such strategies.

Her body couldn't lie. So by the time Theo arrived at the shop, she laid it all out.

"Look, I don't really understand what happened last night and I'm not sure what to do with it. But I realize that I really like you. Though I don't know what that means." She paused.

He smiled and said," Well, I more than like you."

The word that he *didn't* speak was 'love'. It was the loudest unspoken word she had ever heard and she wasn't so sure what to do with that. She wasn't sure if it was a good thing or a bad thing. She kind of wished her body could do the thinking and talking for her again because her head was spinning, struggling.

She tried to continue, "And if we were to actually start dating or something, I don't know...You know what my life is right now."

She wasn't sure what she was hoping for. If he were to say "Hey you're right, this is bad timing, let's not go there" would she be relieved or upset?

Instead he responded with, "Let's take it one day at a time, okay?" As much as he wished to be able to soothe her fears, he knew there were no guarantees. As much as he wished to be part of her life, he didn't want to be 'that guy', coming in after a break up only to be left behind again after her heart had healed.

They talked for hours and when he left, they shared another kiss. And though she knew there was no going back, she wished she had a clearer vision of what was to happen going forward.

That night, she dreamed she was trying to leave her house. She was sitting in the driveway in her pickup truck and it was snowing. Her ex pulled in behind her, trapping her there. She was angry and emotional. Theo opened the passenger side door and got in. She yelled at him, "Get out. It's not safe!".

"I'm getting in. Let's go".

"Suit yourself", she said as he climbed in. Looking around to plan her escape, the last thing she said was "You'd better buckle up". Then, she spun her tires through the snow-covered yard and erratically drove away at top speed.

She woke up thinking, 'One day at a time.' as she reached for her phone.

CHAPTER 19

The coals were finally burning down and LaVieauna took the last of the cookies out of the oven. She had spent a good deal of the day making these last batches and while she usually got up early to bake breads and other more delicate things, this was different. This 'cookie' was for stopping 'the wasting disease'.

She had to make it after the store closed because 'Tirggel' or Dirgelli as her mother had called it, had to bake at a higher heat then the other confections. It was also a way to conceal what she was doing as the cookies were considered a 'heresy' due to the special molds used to invoke the saints. They were considered 'graven images' and only men who belonged to 'guilds could make them as licensed by the Church. LaVieauna's molds had no saints but were each a square from the Tarrochio higher Arcana. Even more heretical.

LaVieauna considered her cookies as the original and theirs, stolen. She saw their laws as silly but the disease was very serious and it was making its evil face known again. It seemed like it was doing a dance with the Pox to see how many people it could kill. This time the disease was hitting the poor part of the town and Tirggel was a curative for the 'wasting' and, Romans be damned, she was making cookies.

The price of the cookie as made only by 'guild' bakers was too costly for the poor. The Church would not be handing them out any time soon. The poor could not afford to live as their tithes were spent to make sure Bishops could walk on slippers of spun gold.

LaVieauna had long had the molds and rollers as her family had been making them long before they were 'saint cakes'. They had been making them when they were called 'Tarrochio' or 'China biscuits' long before the men had stolen them for their bakeries. Her little wooden hand carved molds had come from Rome before Geneva was even a Christian village.

Her mother had told her that her family had come up from Sicily as a Commedia dell'Arte troupe but they were really 'Gypsiennes' who hid their medicines in the 'saint' cookies. Her mother had told her that their Dirgelli was so old that it had originally come all the way from Cathay, a cure for the plague and various other diseases depending on the herbs and the images that were pressed into it.

She had, oddly, received a note from the Mother Abbess in town who had just been in the day before requesting a secret batch be made. She would pick it up at midnight. This night. It was almost midnight now. The cookies, made in very hot ovens, were cooling down to become the hard, sweet, spicy biscuits that healed.

She looked at the garish Swiss bracket clock her husband had sent from Basel where he had been sent to broker a peace with the Prussians threatening to annex the northern reaches of the canton. His being a soldier solicitor afforded her the privilege of her dream to be a baker but her real talent and passion was to be a healer and make the 'little saints', only men were allowed to make. Legally.

She hoped that when her husband returned, she would see if perhaps she could get an exception to the rule since the poor and the foreign so badly needed her skills and she, by rights, at least in her opinion, had been making the cookies long before the laws were enacted.

As the clock chimed, she heard the knock at the door and imagined the Mother Abbess in a great hurry to knock so loud. She ran toward the door, just as it was kicked open. Red coated Gendarmes filed into her store, running past her to her ovens. As they passed, she knew that she had been entrapped and she already knew who would be coming in next. "Good evening, Fraulein." His smirking superior face had changed little since her days as a military wife at the barracks, in the days before her husband had become an officer.

She curtsied stiffly. "Herr Bishop…" She neglected to use honorifics just as he refused to speak French or Latin to her.

"I am sure that you have guessed by now my little ruse. Forgive me, but your Mother Abbess was unable to send the note herself as she was arrested as soon as she left your shop yesterday."

"May I ask on what charge?"

"No, you may not ask, but I will tell you anyway." He was enjoying this too much. "The Sisters of the Dominican Order of Travelers are accused of witchcraft and we have your little cookies in her possession as proof. You too are under arrest."

"My husband will not allow this." She protested as two soldiers grabbed her arms roughly

"Your husband, Fraulein, is quite dead." he oddly bowed as he said this. "You do know that it was I who sent him North? I'm afraid that he never got as far as Basel. It seems that he stopped to pay his respects in Chauvet and was killed in your family chapel. Pity. Seems a very unfortunate fire.

LaVieauna felt all the air leave her body in a rush. She couldn't breathe. But the sudden ringing in her ears did little to block out his continued words.

"The Lord saith, you know…" He gestured above. She looked at her clock on the wall, wondering if he were lying. "What I do thou knowest not now; but thou shalt know hereafter."

She heard the clock again and he smirked. "Oh, the clock… I sent you the clock. I could have given you so much more."

"Not happiness." She choked out the words as her heart froze and she fought the urge to spit at him.

"Well, only the Lord giveth happiness. But I can take it away."

He signaled his men to come out from the kitchen. "You are to be escorted to Monruz where you will collect your daughter and hand her over to me. Your store is forfeit to the Church and you will be put to death with the rest of the sisters upon your return." He added mockingly, "Of course, you will be given a trial first."

The soldiers had confiscated the cookies and brought them to the Bishop. He took one and ate it as if it were just a confection and not a cure. "You realize that your daughter is now the same age as you were when you first refused my… offer? She will not be given that choice." He took one more cookie and left her store.

She was brusquely grabbed by the soldiers who walked her to the door. As soon as the Bishop was out of sight, one of them whispered, "Run. Go to Motta, Madame. The Dominicans will give you Sanctuary."

"But I am not a nun!"

"You will be. It is your only chance. Your husband was our friend. Run!"

She ran through the night and was at Motta by morning. Exhausted and heartbroken, she was greeted by the Mother Abbess who thought her to have been jailed. As she wept in her arms, the Abbess whispered, "We still have friends in Rome. The Holy Father has granted you Sanctuary if you will take your vows with us. We are tertiary but are now prisoners of these walls. We will be safe here though, as long as the Archbishop honors these papers."

"I fear he will not be stopped by a piece of parchment with a drop of wax pressed on it. His vendetta is against me, and personal."

"I swear to you, sister, he will not bother you here or your daughter in Monruz. He is bound by forces stronger than paper and older than the ways of men." The Abbess removed a woven leather cord and pulled a black figure from her habit and placed it over LaVieauna's head. "You are now one of us. Terra Stella, my daughter. May you be Blessed in Her Name as you are Healed in Her Name and I will do my best to Teach you in Her Name. For the Love of God…"

LaVieauna wept. She was finally Home.

ABSINTHE, ALEWIVES & ALCHEMY

CHAPTER 20

Catherine sat bolt upright in her bed. She quickly looked around to see if anyone else was awake and wiped tears she knew would be there. "Teach in Her name. Heal in Her name. Bless in Her name." Hearing those words spoken by someone else pulled her back into her own memory as if the dream had awakened her for a purpose.

She remembered way back when her children were just entering school age laying in her bed one morning and hearing those words. No loud booming voice from God. No angelic choirs or shining light. The sun did not break through the clouds, no angel choirs sang. Just a firm voice that was not from within or from without. Simple. 'Teach in her name. Heal in her name. Bless in her name.'

It had an immediate impact on her and it was to become her 'Charge'. The questions, the search, the wanting to have a store had all started not long after. But after hearing it in the dream, she realized that it had existed long before, almost as if it had been hidden in her own DNA.

Maybe it was there all along and she just hadn't been able to hear it. Back then, she felt like it was a command to teach, heal and bless others but seeing LaVieauna in her dream she realized that she was the one that needed teaching, healing and blessing. She knew that she had been searching, researching and scrambling to help everyone else. That was her way.

As it was, the voice itself was powerful partly because she was finally able and ready to hear it. She just had not heard it as a personal protection order. It took having a persecutor to realize that she was the one that needed help first and that she wasn't to be everyone else's savior.

Teach. Heal. Bless. It seemed so simple as a 'mission' statement but she had not realized that she saw herself as a missionary. It was really more of a prescription. Take one of each and call me in the morning. When she rethought her original interpretation of her 'charge' she began to rethink other things, like her idea of in whose name she was teaching, healing and blessing. She thought she knew who 'Her' was and now she wasn't so sure.

Was she an archetype? Or just a group" Or was She the mother of all Goddesses? Or her Mother? Was she like the Eve of goddesses from some primordial goddess garden? She felt emotional at her realizations.

As she wiped her eyes, she also realized that she still had yesterday's makeup on and it was making her eyes sting. Most mornings, it was stinging eyes or full bladders that got her up to face the day and she realized that these, like everything else in her life, were external forces that compelled her. She had no impeller. Much less a rudder.

Like Cat, LaVieauna also lived in service of others and she had the sense that owning a bakery was just a stepping stone to what she would really become if she allowed herself to be taught, to be healed and to be blessed. What if the store was also just a stepping stone? She closed her eyes to try to avoid this thought as well as to avoid getting up before her kids needed her. She needed to soak in the last moments of rest that she could.

She rubbed her eyes. It stung. She looked at her hand it was black with soot. Her eye watered and she was about to get up to wash when she realized that she was sitting on a cave floor. Cleanly swept, flat but still, a cave floor. The morning sun was streaming in. She wiped her brow and moved her stringy hair out of her face. She blew the errant hair that had fallen back across her eye as her hands were palms together on a bone handle attached to a leather cord around her neck. She began to twirl it quickly into a piece of black stone with a prayer-like intensity.

It was soft like wood and she held it clenched between her bare heels as she patiently drilled a hole into it. 'It' was a small figure less than two inches long. A stylized body with no arms or head, just a torso with a large buttocks and tiny feet. She drilled the hole until it started to smoke then she flipped the figure over to drill it from the other side.

At her feet were a dozen more of the carved figures along with a few other shapes, all with holes drilled into them. As she looked out at the sun rising, she heard a low growl behind her, it grew louder and more insistent.

"Hush. I'm almost done. The fish aren't even awake yet." Another growl. Without looking back, she got up and wiped her hands on a piece of fur as a large bear slipped in beside her. She patted the bear's head and walked into the morning sunlight. She tucked the awl she had just used in between her breasts and walked down to the lake below the caves. As she looked back, she noticed none of the other women were up.

"Good. Let's get some fish." The bear grumbled its approval and it was now she who was following. "Slow down. You men are all alike." She laughed at her own joke as she broke into a jog to catch up. At the river, the bear waded in carefully as the woman went upstream to slap the water and chase the fish to him.

Within minutes the bear had caught a fish and the woman patted him on the head as he released it to her. She grabbed her awl and swiftly ran it through the fish's eyes and laid it on the shore. The bear had already caught another and was about to offer it to her but the first one was so big she signed for him to go ahead and eat it. The bear sat down right where he was and began feasting with a delicateness that you would not expect from such a large animal.

While he ate, the woman scanned the sandy shore for sand bubbles and pulled up a dozen clams with her stick and rinsed them off. She cracked one open and the bear came over to eat the inside. He gave the shell to her and they headed back to the cave. Once there, she staked the fish on a stick and buried the clams next to the fire in the fire pit. She blew gently on the fire but it was dead so she grabbed some dried riverweed and her awl and drilled into a piece of driftwood until it smoked. She carefully fed it the fibrous weed and blew it until a flame caught the dried weeds then she carefully placed them under the kindling she had gathered. As it crackled to life, she added more wood until she had a large fire going. The sun was pouring in now and the fire helped illuminate the cave.

All over the walls were dozens of animals drawn in charcoal and ochres in varying shades of yellow and reddish brown. The woman looked over at a blank part of cave wall, grabbed a piece of charred wood and carefully darkened a series of dots on the wall she had made the night before and sat back to look at it. The bear settled in next to her and stared at the wall with her. After a few moments, the woman grabbed the piece of charcoal and lightly, quickly drew a large Oryx around the dots. Then, mixing Ochre with tallow, she began to paint in long arching strokes as she added lines, shading and detail to the large beast.

As she moved her whole body to create the mural, Cat realized that she was now painting with or, maybe, as the woman. She could feel the strong and long strokes and she realized that she was painting a constellation.

She heard the song coming from her as it echoed in the cave and the bear swayed to and fro as if it were in a trance. As the woman outlined the animal once more in a dark charcoal, she finished her song and backed up to look at her handiwork.

Satisfied, she went down to the stream to wash but on the way there she encountered several honeybees in the low ground cover full of small white flowers. She made note of their flight path and when the last one left, she ran after it. It flew in a straight line where the others had flown previously and led her to an old, rotting tree by the river. As she looked up into the bare branches, she saw the giant beehive and the swarm bristled in answer as if it had seen her too.

She carefully backed away and ran to the cave. There, she wrapped an old fur on a long stick. She lit it on fire and brought the smoking, foul smelling stick to the hive. She dropped it underneath and quickly harvested the bitter herbs that grew by the river and lit them on fire. She smelled the bitter smoke of the healing herbs now forcing the bees to leave in a huge swarm. She draped the burning fur on the branch and the branch caught fire as the last few bees exited the folds of the hive.

When the fur went out, the woman broke the branch where the fire had weakened it and she held the hive aloft. As she did this, she saw her bear ambling down, nose in the air having been awakened from his nap by the smell of honey. As she walked back to the cave, the bear walked slowly behind her. She walked to the back of the cave and laid the hive down on a flat expanse of rock.

She grabbed some ochre dust and placed her hand on the wall and blew the red dust all over her hand leaving a reverse stencil. She looked above the handprints that lined the bottom of the cave wall and looked at a tiny cluster of dots surrounded by the figure of a woman's torso that had no arms or head. She bowed low and grabbed her own little figurine she wore around her neck. She rubbed it in her long hair a few times and then touched it between her breasts until she felt a familiar tiny shock. The bear leaned up against her and she smiled. She broke off a shelf like piece of hive and they walked back to the fire to eat the fish and clams along with a rare treat.

That night, the woman watched as the other women came out of the caves and greeted her with a nod. No one spoke as they all waited for the sun to completely set, then they watched the great star animals appear and circle the night sky. On nights that were clear and moonless like this, they watched for the signs and watched for the stars to arise that were to signal the gathering season. As the small and not especially bright handful of stars arose in a little cluster they began to sing.

Cat did not understand the song but she knew a lament when she heard one and she decided that they were waiting for someone to come home. As they sang, she realized that the little cluster of stars was the 'Seven Sisters' and they were singing about 'home'.

The dream was so real that when she awoke, she half expected to smell the smoke and fish and to be chewing on waxy honeycomb. After she had awakened sufficiently from this dream, she realized that she had been somewhere before time was time.

She recognized the beautiful animals on the cave walls as she had seen many like them in magazines and documentaries but she had never considered that they might be constellations. It seemed obvious now. Even though they were in positions 50,000 years different from today's night sky.

If goddesses were worshipped by religions then this must be the mothers of those mothers. 'Her' Mothers. The ones before religions. She felt as if these women who lived in the caves were waiting for these nameless faceless 'GrandMothers' to return. A time when Grandmothers and Goddesses were one without any words or rules to divide them. A time before the Great Mother of All, there was simply All. Before there was a 'seated one'. Before there was a seat. A sign. Or even a Sound...

A voice so old that it made no sound. If the Big Bang were real, there was no air on which sound waves could travel. No energy upon which light could travel. There would not possibly have been a 'Bang' at all. Like the voice that had first quietly told her to Teach, Heal and Bless it would have suddenly been where it had not been before and then waited billions of years to be finally heard. The most profound event in the universe would have come into existence in complete silence. That was Her. She was there before the Alpha and would be there long after the Omega.

Cat lay there taking this all in as the alarm buzzed quietly, she whispered, 'For the love of god...'. She meant it.

ABSINTHE, ALEWIVES & ALCHEMY

CHAPTER 21

Though Cat's marriage was over, she was often still afraid. She was, however, getting stronger and she had begun to increasingly stand up for herself and for her girls. Her ex continued to challenge her, control her, and try to stop her from succeeding, but it was becoming more frequent that his tactics no longer worked.

Frustrated that his strategies were not having an effect, his anger grew. He was becoming increasingly unhinged and continued to threaten her and try to take away anything he thought might be of value. It was obvious he had reached his breaking point when he finally levied his ultimate threat, to take away her life.

She had pulled into the parking lot of the apartment complex, texted her daughter that she was there to pick them up and saw Marie look out the window. Cat waved to her, but she responded by ducking quickly back behind the curtain. Her first clue that something was up. Her oldest texted back that they would be right down. Instead, it was their father who exited the building.

He came to her car window and started to scream at her. "Bitch, did you have fun fucking him all weekend?" his face was red and he was shaking with rage.

She held the steering wheel at two and ten looking straight ahead. "Where are the girls?" was all she asked.

His demeanor was beyond threatening this time. His energy was always scarier than his words. The rage would ripple off of him in waves and the look in his eyes changed in a way that made her understand he was on the edge of snapping. "You're just a lying whore. I did everything for you. I gave you everything."

Her voice shook but she did her best to sound firm. "Look, you need to stop and my girls better be down here right now or I'm calling the police." she reached for her phone on the seat next to her. He reached in through the window and grabbed it out of her hand. She saw her daughter look out the window again and fear gripped her. "Not this time" she thought "It's different now" the mantra kicked in trying to override, or at least stem the flow of adrenaline running through her veins.

"Give me my phone" she said slowly and as calmly as possible.

"You fucking bitch, I will kill you *and* your boyfriend. You won't even see it coming. I'll sneak in while you're sleeping and shoot you both in the head." The images came quickly then. The flash of a knife, the cut of a sword, the hand smashing a head against rock. She couldn't breathe, she felt darkness, she was drowning.

"Use your Magic." The voice came firm and loud from within her. With a sharp intake of breath, she pulled herself up taller. She looked him in the eyes and suddenly had an odd memory of a time that he had yelled at her for carrying a pizza box wrong. Something had come over her then and in a flash of anger, she threw the pizza box down and stared fiercely at him. Whatever had come over her then had come over her now. It was only for a second but that was enough as she looked him in the eye now.

He stepped back and suddenly threw the phone at her and stormed back inside with no word or cursory glance toward the girls who had come down the stairs and out into the parking lot. As he stormed away, her fear and adrenaline returned but something had just happened in that moment, she was sure. She tried to pull herself together for her daughters' sake. They were already upset from their weekend there and from the little that they had already witnessed from the upstairs apartment window. She was so upset she thought she might vomit but she was determined to hold it together and to get home safe.

"But it's different now. It's different now. This time, I'll survive." The mantra repeated through her head.

The following day she shared the incident with Theo. She was still shaken and feeling way over adrenalized.

He told her that she should be proud of herself but suggested that she take out a personal protection order against him. It felt weird to do so. As much as she had seen and experienced, for some reason there was a reluctance to act. Fear? Conditioning? Enculturation? Whatever it was, she pulled together enough courage to make her way to the courthouse to file all the paperwork, endure the questioning and recount the story.

After having to recount that day to the police, she shared her memory of the 'pizza incident' with Theo and he said that memory was a kind of magic. Like method acting. Like remembering dreams or past lives. She liked that. Dreaming and memory as magic was a much better theory than insanity. And he was right. She was getting stronger and braver, even if she didn't always feel it.

After that, Theo joined Cat and her daughters more and more often. Her kids had met him, originally, at the store and liked him right away. It seemed a natural transition when he started stopping by the house. They would spend casual evenings just hanging out together, watching t.v. or eating good food. Theo was an amazing cook. His relaxed manner put all of them at ease. It was so good for them to be able to laugh and have some fun.

For the first time in her life, she wasn't feeling alone. For the first time, she felt as if she had a true partner. Still, they avoided too much talk of the future. They continued to take things day by day. He was all too aware of the pressures both she and her daughters were under.

He would always listen, often offer advice, most often, a story and, sometimes, just steady arms with which to hold her when her world was full of craziness. She realized she had never known this type of love. She realized it was exactly the kind she had always wanted but it only seemed to exist in fairy tales. Fairy tales. Her dreams were making her rethink her understanding of fairy tales. Like memories, they were a type of magic.

They were cleaning up after dinner at her home one evening. Her children were gone that weekend. She had been particularly depressed about it so Theo had stopped by to cook for her. He'd also brought a bottle of wine.

Feeling full in so many ways and warm from the wine, they laughed as they did the dishes together. She reached over to embrace him, kissed him softly and became suddenly serious as she announced, "I'm going to marry you".

It was one of her 'knowings' and it came unbidden to her mind and unedited to her mouth. Once it was out, she didn't even care. She knew it to be the truth. How odd it was to her to speak out loud one of the truths of her heart. Only a short time ago she would have been terrified at the prospect. But within that short time, she had faced many terrifying prospects. Embracing love didn't seem so scary anymore. Plus, this 'knowing' was a glimpse of the future she could finally see. It felt as if they had always been together, were supposed to be together. It was only natural that they would be again. He smiled at her, laughed quietly and simply answered, "Okay."

Still, there were more pressing real-life issues to which they both needed to attend. Theo began working for her at the store while she worked another job to pay rent. Second jobs were increasingly common as the economy slipped into a deep recession.

The shops all around her were closing. 'Going out of business' signs were becoming a common site. Her store was one of the few remaining on the street that no one much bothered to venture down anymore. All of her troubles hit long before it seemed to find its way to society. Now that it had filtered to the masses, the seriousness of its effects was weighing heavily on her mind.

It seemed surreal that only a few months before, Theo had submitted her name to a business organization, filled out paperwork and garnered multiple letters of referral, winning her the prestigious statewide Small Business "Retailer of the Year" award. Things had been looking up.

She was making good connections, meeting fascinating people. Her curious dreams and synchronicities had not been slowing. She was still in survival mode and still trying to figure out all the pieces of this crazy puzzle. Yet, within all the chaos, she was beginning to feel less hopeless and more determined.

She began to feel those same 'sisters' who had visited her all those years ago, come to visit her again. They seemed to empathize with her but they also seemed to be pushing her in a new direction. Her dreams had awakened childhood memories and things she had covered and hidden. She started to make her own oil blends for health and for magic. She began to blend teas and read the leaves. Again. It wasn't, so much, like learning. She was remembering.

Then one day she opened an email from her Aunt Henrietta. Her aunt had sent her a documentary about the history of Absinthe. She was curious as to why her aunt had passed this on to her. Her only clue was the cryptic message at the top, "Did you know this?"

Cat sat down and followed the link to a video. It was interesting enough. It made her think about the Absinthe tea she had begun to make for upset stomachs. Still, she wasn't sure why it was sent. About half-way through, it hit her. The narrator spoke of Couvet in Switzerland, he spoke of a Mere Henriod and her daughters, and the mystery of who was the first to make Absinthe.

Cat jumped up from her chair. She had flashes of the shop they showed her years ago, she saw her 'sisters' who had visited her. They weren't actual sisters but sisters of a different sort. She even felt a flash of emotion for her 'Mother' so long now gone. They were her family, they were her ancestors! They were real. And so was the mystery of who really invented Absinthe.

She had a strange sense of deja vu. She had a strange sense of vindication and purpose. She knew this not to be a coincidence but yet another piece. She just wasn't sure how it fit. It was so hard to focus on anything making sense while she was fighting for survival, still fighting against harassment and threats, still fighting in the courts, still fighting for her daughters.

She had hoped that things were turning around. She was hoping to survive the recession. She hung on for a year after the divorce, but without her business loan it was only a matter of time before she had to close her shop for good. There was simply too much stacked against her, nationally, in her business neighborhood and personally. She was in survival mode. She had to stay safe, to regroup to figure out how to navigate all the changes and challenges in her life.

The only thing she knew for sure was that this part of her life, like so many others, was over. She felt numb. There were too many unknowns. But one thing she did know, was that Theo was there for her, and he was in it for the long haul.

They had already been through so much together in a seemingly short amount of time. They had been together for over a year now and she was once again learning how to trust and, despite everything that had happened, she was allowing herself to hope.

She thought about her dream of Isis that she'd had, now seemingly so long ago. She could still see all those bloody, cut up limbs and body parts laying before the Goddess. That was her life. She had to put all the pieces together. That, she thought, was how she had assembled her store. Putting this with that, learning as she went and adding and subtracting, piece by piece.

Isis had tasked her with that, in her own life and showed her how, told her that she not only had the ability, but that she must use it. She felt a bit like Dr. Frankenstein, digging up pieces of the past from graves long forgotten. She had assembled her store in the same way. She wondered if her more organic approach had killed it and wondered what that meant for her life.

She knew that she had approached the whole store idea 'piece-meal' and told Theo that maybe that was why she had to close. He said that 'piece-meal' meant 'measure by measure' and that the word for 'measure' and 'wheat' were the same. His picture of 'piece meal' was like adding a little flour to your starter every day, measure by measure. When you ran out of harvest wheat, you simply switched to winter wheat.

The store, he thought, was not her destiny but a piece of it, a measure that had kept them alive until the next step. No more Winter wheat. What would she feed her sourdough now?

Theo had no answers but he helped her pack up her store and close it during a terrible winter storm, taking several trips in their van, late into an icy cold night. The last load was so full that Theo tied the back-lift gate with an old extension cord hoping it would hold long enough to make it to their new house.

"I'll give you a moment with your 'baby' and go lock up the back." He hugged her and disappeared around the corner.

She closed the door on the empty shop and looked at her mural through the window one last time and read "I am the beauty of the green earth, and the white moon among the stars". She had no idea of what was next but she knew that it was time to move on.

She thought about the 'Charge of the Goddess', where that quote had come from. The next line of the Charge came to her as she remembered. "...I call unto thy soul: Arise and come unto me..." Her immediate thought was 'Tell me where you are and I will...' More than anything, she wished that she had a 'Charge' that was more like a map than a riddle.

Theo came back around and handed her the keys after locking the back door and taking out the last trash. She slipped the keys into the mail slot, took a deep breath to steady her nerves and said a silent goodbye to her shop. It had taught her so much, healed her so much and blessed her with their new life together.

As she walked hand in hand with Theo to their van which was filled as if they were going on a long trip, she handed Theo the keys and said, "I wish I knew where we were going…"

"Home, I guess…"

"No, I mean after all of this." She thought about the words on the wall again. When she painted it, they were the only words of that whole charge that spoke to her. They still did.

She was remembering the day she painted it and was about to say to Theo, 'Remember...' but as she started the sentence it occurred to her that her memories were magic and that 're-membering' was to put the pieces together. She 'remembered' her little 'Isis' as she pressed the little black 'Venus' against her heart and walked slowly to the van. As she got in, Theo looked at her and smiled. "Ready to make some magic?"

He was trying to cheer her up. "If I knew what it was..." She didn't want to be cheered up.

"You'll remember. You probably need some pizza. We'll stop and get some and I'll let you hold it any way you like."

She smiled. Memory really was magic...

CHAPTER 22

Cat was a firm believer in Destiny. Capital 'D'. She also believed that if you weren't doing what you were supposed to be doing with your life, then you would be taken out. Someone else would be put in your stead. She hoped that "taken out" wasn't literal, because she knew she wasn't yet living her purpose but she was trying. She wondered how many 'try's she would get?

Sometimes the ancestors she felt around her seemed impatient and frustrated that she didn't seem to be understanding all their 'clues'. Often, she would cry and be angry and yell out to them, "Just tell me what I'm supposed to do! I'll do it, I swear!"

Theo had moved in with her and her daughters as soon as they were able to find a place large enough for all five of their children, his and hers. Being together in this way allowed for more late-night talks, and more 'life planning sessions. As Theo helped talk her through her own life path, they worked together to figure out these clues and these dreams.

As they did, they realized with increasing clarity, that they were supposed to be together, all of them, for so many reasons. Sometimes, she almost felt like the spirits she worked with had set her up. But she didn't mind being 'set up' in this way. This time, it had led her to someone good. She was sure they would lead her now to some*thing* good. But what? She had this nagging feeling she needed to understand something, to do something. It always seemed to linger on the edges of her awareness.

She was getting more regular visits now. She remembered this feeling growing up when she could often see the spirits, family long past or other weird phenomena. But it made her nervous to actually see them, so she mostly blocked it out. However, she was never quite able to block out the ability to hear and to know. She stifled it for a long time, but it seemed to be back in force now that so many things had changed in her life.

The two that seemed to 'pop in' the most now were the women she thought of as 'her sisters'. The ones who encouraged her to open her shop and even gave her the name. She thought maybe she had disappointed them. They seemed so excited with what she was doing at the time. Her store had failed but they were still with her. They would guide her when she was blending her herbs, making tisanes or extracts. Often, they would give her tips as to what to try instead of what she was using, or tell her to cut this leaf but tear that one. Sometimes with words but, more often, they seemed to find it easier to take her hand or turn her head.

They'd offer advice as to which seeds or plants she needed to boil and which ones were those that should be soaked in oil or alcohol. Sometimes she thought she must be crazy, standing in her kitchen, listening to dead people. But she was learning a lot, including how to trust her intuition.

What she couldn't learn there, would come to her in dreams. Her dreams were coming fast and furious now. She was beginning to fill her shelves with different teas and tins of healing herbs. Sometimes it felt like she was living one life when she was awake, and then, another life after she fell asleep.

He walked into the dining room tying on yet another new cravat. She wasn't sure if it was his voice or simply his presence that annoyed her more. "I think you're getting a bit carried away with all of… this" he said with a sweeping motion to the various herbs, ointment jars and extracts. They had, along with stills and cookers, been taking over the kitchen of their home and were now spilling into the built-ins of their once formal dining room.

"Carried away? This is who I am. This is what I do. It's what I've always done." Her tone was mildly clipped and formal. She corrected herself. "We have always done. Or do you forget where you came from?" Her tone was now more polite but pointed.

"Look, Suzanne, we are not in a position to be hosting 'tea parties' until all hours of the night. Especially the kind you do. The people coming through here are not necessarily those with whom we can be seen. Society simply doesn't work that way. Not anymore. These are not your grandmother's times."

She answered him with a cool side glance. He had purchased the hotel with what she felt to be rather 'suspicious money'. She certainly had no idea where it came from. Between his gambling friends, his drinking vigilante friends and his sudden interest in distilling alcohols, she wondered what kind of hotel, he had envisioned; a brothel perhaps? She held her tongue.

He knew that even though she had been brought up in a certain class and a certain family, she was still all too comfortable in the old country ways. She passed no judgement on others, just, perhaps, him. He sometimes wished he had known this before they were arranged to be married. As a Motta, they were practically cousins. Then he thought, 'as if that matters.'

Knowing that he would never be able to squelch what he viewed as her eccentricities, he decided he could at least distance himself from it. "I have made arrangements for you to move these...things...and your 'salon' to my aunt's place. She is getting on in years and you can help her with her own country bumpkin crafts. You are to move your supplies to my grandfather's and I have arranged for you to have your teas with his spinster sister there from now on. I trust that you will find it a more suitable atmosphere than at my hotel."

Having a new salon was not what Suzanne Henriod had in mind. She was already independently wealthy. She also knew that her husband, a local vigilante, was desperate to legitimize her to preserve his own reputation. Politics were shifting and he was feeling the stress of trying to fit in, becoming increasingly nervous and neurotic. People were gossiping, saying they had a 'white marriage' despite the fact that they had several children.

And while she adored her eccentric 'Tante Melle', she did not relish the idea of becoming her caretaker. But, in the end, the move turned out quite well. She soon found out that her husband's aunt needed no caretaker at all and was in fact, an endless font of knowledge. She already had her own 'tea salon' that was suspiciously held in the room housing her brother's still.

She had expected to lose some of her regulars but it was quite the opposite. This was a far more hospitable place to share tea. Within a few years Suzanne knew everything and everyone in her auntie's 'business', including the fact that it was more than a business. Her aunt was called 'Les Sages' by the women of the various communities. This wasn't an official title but women who had memory and knowledge of the old ways or were otherwise gifted were often called that. Suzanne noticed that many of the women who gathered around the elder Henriod were 'Les Sages' or 'Wise Women' and were also a part of her aunt's secret sisterhood.

It was not long before Suzanne Henriod had herself joined the 'Sisterhood of the Hives' and, over the years, when 'Melle' became more and more unable to manage the making of elixirs, she gave the title of 'Melle' to Suzanne, as it had been given to her many years before. Most people assumed that it was a diminutive for 'Mademoiselle' but to the ladies of the Salon Henriod, it was the highest honor a woman of Val de Travers could be given.

The new 'Melle' didn't care too much for the actual "business" end of her business. That seemed to take care of itself. What she really enjoyed was trading ingredients from afar and learning new techniques from a wide variety of other women engaged in what she liked to think of as 'magical food'. Wines, breads, cheeses, kefirs and other 'living foods' were available to her as she lived in the intensely multicultural little town of Couvet that had a fortuitous confluence of cultures that loved 'cultures'.

Along with her herbals and tinctures, her version of the original Absinthe became the one that the apothecarists and distillers were trying to copy and steal. Even her own husband had asked her more than once to divulge his aunt's secret recipe.

Cat's elbow slipped out from under her chin and her head almost hit the desk as she startled herself awake. She had fallen asleep while reading the latest spate of emails all the while avoiding looking at a government website on how to declare bankruptcy without a lawyer. She had fallen asleep frustrated with the fact that she was actually too poor to be bankrupt. "If I could afford a damn lawyer, I wouldn't need to be doing this!"

Now she was orienting herself in the darkness that had settled over the room as she slept. She could still feel on her own hands the indentations of rings on the fingers of the woman in her dream. Rings of wealth and connection on the left, and her more secret sacred connections on her right hand.

She was comforted by her own 'real life' right hand as she touched her 'ring of Isis' that she wore as a promise to be faithful to the Goddess. She checked her left ring finger, now missing 'the ring of ownership', she used to call her wedding band. Instead, she wore her beloved heavy gold snake ring that she had had made for herself.

It took her a moment to separate her own feelings about her ex from those of Suzanne's feelings for her husband. She knew that the younger 'Melle' had a strained marriage but she didn't sense fear or loathing in her. There was an odd indifference, a feeling that her marriage was a convenience contracted by the families.

Cat sensed that Melle the elder and the younger were quite happy doing what they did and Cat knew that she was probably projecting as she had always wanted a partner and mate with which she could share her own magical leanings. She was very happy that Theo liked doing things with her. Including parenting.

"Hey" Theo had entered the room. "Why don't you wrap up for the night, come to bed. I've already tucked everyone else in. It's your turn." He smiled, a smile full of love and concern as well as his own exhaustion. She wasn't sure when life was going to get easier, but it helped to know she didn't have to navigate it alone.

Cat shutdown the laptop and reached for Theo as the blue glow of the screen went dark. Her favorite part of the day was the end of it. She curled up against him in bed, his arm wrapped around her and she breathed deep as the warm skin on skin and beating of his heart lulled her back to sleep.

There was a knock at the back of her shoppe. It didn't surprise her, a knock so late in the evening. Often, those who needed help but couldn't afford to be seen visiting her shop by day, ventured out past dark. "Bon Soir, Madame Henriod"

"Reverend Baillod!" Melle was rarely caught off guard but this was quite the surprise. Because her husband was so well respected it wasn't long before the more conservative bourgeoisie beat a path to her door (often incognito, at night or by emissary) and it was they who 'paid the rent' while most 'business' at the shoppe were women who were bartering and sharing the fruits of their labor. But to see the Reverend himself, was most unusual.

"I must admit I am surprised to see you. Please, come in." She stepped aside to let him enter. Her back room was filled with drying herbs, little clay pots waiting to be filled, bottles of liquids of every color imaginable and on a table in a corner, obscured by the tools of her craft, was a statue of a seated woman facing a bear. He took it all in quickly with intelligent eyes, leaving him seemingly more nervous than before.

"I'm here on behalf of my little brother" he paused then added quickly," I understand you might be able to help. He has been ill for weeks. He is losing weight, he can't eat, he suffers from dysentery, he is feverish. I have tried everything. Might you have something… here" he motioned toward her bottle lined shelves, "that could perhaps, help?"

Melle heard the desperation in his voice. She didn't know too much about the newest leader of the oldest Catholic church in town. But she did know he cared for his youngest brother like a son. He was roughly her same age, certainly young enough to have living parents. But she also knew there was much unrest in neighboring France and many were crossing into Switzerland to find a new start after tragedy and loss.

"I can help." Melle answered matter of factly, then turned and reached for one of the little bottles of green liquid near the statue of the woman and the bear. "Mix a spoonful of this with some cold spring water and honey, 3 times a day until gone."

"Bless you." he sighed in relief.

"Your blessings don't work here, Father. I'm afraid the Holy Father doesn't approve of me or my kind. Save them for your brother." she smiled and curtsied.

He seemed to relax then and laugh a bit with her. "Then, 'Merci', it is." He smiled squeezing her hand. She noticed and held his gaze a little longer than what one would consider proper. All propriety had already been lost, however, as soon as he had entered her shop, through the back entrance, alone, at night.

At the 'hive' meeting next morning, she was relieved to hear that the gossip that day was of the uprisings in France and about one of the newer residents in Couvet who had been, yet again, scandalized.

"Do tell us Lady Melle, what do you think of your new neighbor?"

Suzanne, the new 'Melle' Henriod, was much more social than her predecessor. As the 'Mellissa' or 'Mellisande' she enjoyed her 'Queen Bee' status amongst the secret hives of women who were locally called 'the Alewives'. A generic term for women who had brewing, fermenting and healing skills as well as ancient skills that were passed down and only shared amongst themselves. It also implied that they all enjoyed gossip and a pint now and then.

The 'Hives' consisted of women who were all leaders in their various communities. There were Jews from Poland and Jennische who had come up from the South, like her Grandfather. Celtic Northerners called Helvetians, 'Ethanikos' or Heathens, women from Greece proper, both Turkey and Anatoly, and other women who represented the original inhabitants of the valley and lakes, called Bärenanbeters or 'Bear Worshippers'. They were the ones who laid claim to having lived there since before the invaders came and why the Canton near Neuchatel was named Bern.

Melle spoke enough of each of their languages to be accepted as one of their own, partly because she actually was related to many, being a Roman Paganis, Roma Sinti and Swiss by ancestry and French, Belgium and Prussian Catholic by marriage.

Her shoppe had become a hub for various women who traded and who kept alive the secret, sacred crafts of their ancestors as well as their various practices, rituals and meanings which they all hid under their feigned Catholicism practiced by men.

"Lady Melle? Your new neighbor? What do you think of him?" the question was repeated. She had been lost in the memory of the night before. She had known of but never officially met the Reverend prior to that evening. She had never expected the strange knowing in her stomach when she saw him. It both disturbed her and saddened her. The only thing she knew for sure was that change was coming. She could taste it on the wind.

"Oh, the 'doctor'." It was not a question but a statement sprinkled with disdain. "Not much. He knows incredibly little for a man purporting to be of the medical profession. I am told that the Constable confiscated his uniform. He is a deserter as well as a fraud. Dubier just needs a cover."

The women gathered there all laughed at her unintended joke but Melle did not find it amusing. "At the behest of my husband, I had been making sure he had some proper medicines with which to stock his bag. It seems they have worked so well that he is gaining more patients but I am losing my own patience as he is constantly badgering my husband for greater supplies. This gives my husband the opportunity to remind me that I am not a doctor."

The women laughed but one of the older ladies present leaned in seriously at that point in the conversation and began to quietly speak, "My Melle", she bowed her head a bit to show respect and continued, "I've seen things. Grave things. You must be careful." Melle jumped at that statement, immediately feeling guilty for the night before. But she'd done nothing wrong! She was about to protest but instead let her continue. The older 'Melle' was known for her gift of 'the sight'.

"Please speak, Tante…" She lowered her gaze in respect but also because she knew of her mentor's extraordinary gifts.

"It has been some years since I passed the bonnet to you. No one suspects that we are more than alewives gossiping and making a few harmless charms and potions. But…" She whispered now. "It's been just Twenty years since I watched my own Tante Anna die, it seems like yesterday. She moved to the city, where we had hoped things would be different for her.

"But, Lady Melle, they are not. They are only better disguised. She was poor, unmarried, a great beauty and a single mother whose only crime was to suffer the death of her child. She did nothing wrong. But she knew things, like we do. She taught the doctor, first as a teacher of cures and then as lovers. When she became pregnant, she refused to end it and he betrayed her. Said he had seen her perform witchcraft and consorted with demons.

"Like us, she could concoct things, she helped people, she knew how to survive on her own." There were tears in her eyes now.

"Forgive me, but you are brazen. Like me, you have status and standing and you have used it to your advantage. But how long will that last? Already those in our town are visiting the doctor and not you. You are losing more than your patience...

"Beware the candles you burn at night cast only one shadow. They say the burning times are over, but there are other ways to kill us." She paused. "You have your daughters to consider."

The room grew very quiet. None of the women there thought of themselves as witches. They simply did as their grandmothers had done. They took care of themselves, their families and their communities. But Melle knew that knowledge was power, and only men were to hold the power in these days. She also understood her aunt's veiled warnings.

The woman who had spoken was the real 'Melle' in her eyes and heart. The one who had taught her. The one who had promised the grimoires back to her when she learned that she was a descendant of Leandro Motta. They were, as all the Motta's and Henriod's, distantly related but these two were related in closer ways. They were sisters of a different sort.

The knowledge that the older 'Melle' had passed on was meant to sustain them financially, but being too financially independent was also a dangerous thing. She was tired of bending to the will of men, bending to the will of the Church, to the will of a Society that, since the Counter-Reforms, was no longer free. Her sister and mentor were right. She had become a little too well known, a little too forward, perhaps she was a little bit brazen.

She thought of her daughters then. She needed to put them first. Before too long they would be of an age to marry. She needed to make sure they had the ability and the means to have some say in their lives. Hopefully more than she had.

"Thank you for your honesty. And my deepest sympathies for the death of our Aunt. I did not know her but I think we should all take heed of your words, Lady Melle."

The old woman bowed low. "You are the Melle now, Lady. I hope you are not the last. Already, the vigilantes are prohibiting me from distilling. I have given my business over to my nephews as I am too old to fight them. You have your station. Your husband is a lieutenant as well and you will be safe as long as the Papists believe your marriage is not white. Forgive my boldness, but we must not pretend that the witch pogroms are over."

The women in the room slowly rose and quietly gathered their things to leave. They didn't speak but with their eyes, each holding each other in spirit and in sisterhood. Before she left, the old woman handed a small bundle of old books to Melle. Melle knew that this would be their last tea together and, for the first time, felt that she was really now 'The Mellissa'.

The Reverend Baillod stopped by the shoppe the next week to share the good news of his brother's recovery. After that, he began to make it a habit and always at obscure times when few if any, would notice his comings and goings. Though he was a man of the cloth, he seemed so different from the pompous Catholic Priests of her husband's Church. His friendliness was making her nervous.

As business-like as she tried to remain, his charm was disarming and she discovered it easy to talk with him for hours. She found herself telling him things she had never told anyone. He always listened without judgement and would often respond with secrets of his own. The more she listened to him, the more convinced she was that he was a pagan in disguise. She would tease him about that and he would laugh but never deny the accusation. There were rumors about 'Trois Maries', the little village on the shores of France where he had come from but he seemed a good Catholic.

Sometimes when he stopped by, she would put him to work. He would help her with preparations, stripping leaves from stems and grinding roots into powders. She would quiz him on the properties of this herb or that. She would then gather her storage jars and he would fill them.

"Ah, now, where is my stool?" She was looking around her supply room for the little step to help her reach a jar on the shelf. "Children! I suppose one of my little imps tucked it somewhere impossible for me to find."

She went ahead, standing on tiptoe, to try to reach it. He came up behind her to help. He reached easily over her head and in doing so pressed up against her back. Once he had the jar in hand, he lowered it down, but did not move from the closeness of her. In fact, he shifted his body in more so that she could feel the entirety of him, the heat, the firmness, his breath. She froze with nowhere to go and no desire to leave that moment.

He put the jar down as she turned to face him. It was not clear if she reached up to him, or he down to her. It didn't matter. Their lips met as his hands moved gently around to the small of her back. She couldn't breathe. She was sure it lasted only a moment but, in that moment, time stopped. She had never been kissed like that before and, she knew, she would never be kissed like that again.

He pulled away suddenly, surprised and ashamed. He apologized repeatedly and left quickly, embarrassed at his transgression. It was all too dangerous, for her more so than for him. How could he have been so foolish? How could he have allowed himself to fall in love? He knew she was married. He knew he should never have been there. Yet he showed up, time and time again, for months.

It was a love he knew could never be realized. That seemed to make it all the more intense. Though he knew he could never allow himself to see her again, he decided that if he could not make her happy, he would do what he could to make sure she was safe.

Melle thought of her Tante's words as she remembered watching the father's shadow pressed up against hers as they moved in the candlelight across the wall. "Brazen, indeed." She thought to herself. "And unbelievably stupid." Her heart was breaking at what she knew could never be. She could never see him again after that. She knew she wouldn't have the will to stay away if she did. Her heart made it crushingly difficult to return to life as she knew it. It was a metaphor for all she knew she must give up.

As the days went by, she missed the Reverend Father's company, his laughter and their conversations more instead of less. She fantasized about what it would be like if they had shared more than just one kiss. She had been trained well and she knew her place. Her place beside her husband. She would manage, somehow. Her concern now had too be the well-being of her daughters.

She needed to listen to her intuition as well as her aunt's warning and be out of the public eye for a while, quite possibly forever. This was a sign. The principality had already passed 'apothecary' laws and guilds were forming that only allowed men to mix and dispense medicine. 'Les Sages' as many local grandmothers of hives were called, were increasingly being accused of witchcraft.

Her intuition was telling her to keep low. She kept her rituals and secrets to herself. She sold her elixirs to apothecarists without labels. She no longer sold to the public. She removed herself, and her daughters from the businesses that were more suspect and only helped those in need through her network of women.

Cat could feel her ancestor's relief and grief as Melle prepared to eventually pass her business to her two older daughters. It was better this way. Someday, they would be able to keep a more normal 'storefront' and would continue to serve the rich women who came for their elixirs. For so many reasons she knew she could no longer be the face of the shop. She trained her young daughters to sell the innocent looking 'waters', candles, soaps and potpourris that only hinted at the entirety of what was made and sold there.

Even her more independent Dominican Sister friends were going back underground. Many of the Bear Women had gone back to their ancestral villages at the foot of the hills, near Val and Monruz where the Church had not yet taken hold with the people.

As 'Melle', she was well respected and loved. Her healing skills were as well-known as her generosity. Her reputation however, wouldn't be enough. Maybe her daughters, who were Catholic, like their father, would fare better. For now, the nearby Dominican Sisters, who ministered to the poor paganry and heathenry, kept her busy in the business of healing. She hoped that if her daughters chose to remain Christians that they would be like her beloved nuns, who she never charged for her elixirs. What was left of the business paid for her ingredients if not her time.

Melle, also began to use her married and more formal name of 'Madame' Suzanne-Marguerite Henriod once again as she did when she had first married Henry-François Henriod IV. Though some still referred to her by 'M'elle' or 'Melle', most assumed it to be only a term of affection. Amid the changing political climate of the new Counter-Reformers, who were bringing back the Inquisition, to take power and wealth from women being called 'Miss' could be dangerous. What would have been humorous just a few years ago now set tongues dangerously wagging even though she had several children. Even 'Mere' or 'Mother' was too 'Sage'.

Meanwhile, Reverend Baillod's church was growing. As was its power within the City Council. He was brought in because he was a charismatic French speaker but the Prussians were slowly taking over his parish. The businesses around her were being increasingly pressured to tithe to the Church, some were being forced to close. Her husband did his best with various bribes to keep this pressure from reaching his hotel, lottery and other scams, but he was losing his patience and what he feared would be his reputation as he increasingly blamed his failings on Melle's 'amusements'.

Her husband had left that morning in a particularly foul mood. She decided to seek solace in her herbal tea and to sit outside behind their kitchen. A young boy slipped around the corner of the house startling her. He bowed. "Mere Henriod?"

"Yes?"

"I've a message for you." with that, he handed her a letter sealed with symbol of the Church. She waited for the boy to leave, then opened it with shaking hands.

My dearest Melle,

I pray you are well and think of you every day. I miss our talks and our time together, regretting every day my weakness in your presence but I cannot regret my love for you. However, I feel responsible for changes in your life and potential danger that I brought to you. I must warn you now of talk within my Church that may affect you and yours. Our elders have been placed in many positions in government, like your husband and Dubier, they are Vigilante and it has become increasingly clear that they will stop at nothing to achieve their goals. Their Avarice makes me fear for their souls but I fear more for your wellbeing.

Your shop has been the subject of many discussions. Your own husband is now the curator of the younger Perronoud's finances and they intend to start a distillery together. They have papers already drawn, accusations at the ready. If you do not conform you will be jailed. To be plain, I suspect there is something of yours that they have, but not completely. Dubied said he bought it from your children and laughed. You may understand this but I heard them talk of potential 'arrangements' that need to be made. I wish I could offer you more than a warning, I am not in a position where I am offered more details of the situation and only wish there were something more I could do. Yours...

It was unsigned. He said all she needed to know. She knew what they wanted and what they had. The purpose of visits to the shoppe by the Major, a friend of her husband's, Perronoud and their neighbor, the doctor were not subtle. Finding her husband was complicit, however, was the final and humiliating missing piece.

She knew by the purchase receipts that they were trying to replicate her Absinthe. They were all too lazy to grow, harvest and dry herbs and she would gladly sell whatever they wanted if it meant keeping her daughters safe, well and fed. That's all that mattered as her sons would inherit everything else. She could lose anything, but not her daughters or the future she had worked hard to give them. But now she knew her husband had tricked her into signing over her inheritance to her daughters so he could sell it himself. She carefully burned the letter in the hearth, sealing her fate. Her decision was made.

Cat woke the next morning feeling as if she hadn't slept at all. She made her coffee extra strong and faced, once again, the antiquated website listing the hoops she would need to jump through to file for bankruptcy herself and, once again, she was wishing she'd gone into law. She also wished that being 'Small Business Owner of the Year' for the entire state came with a cash prize or a trophy she could melt down for gold. Or, at least, a tiara.

She thought about her dream that morning and about how 'Madame Henriod' and 'Melle Henriod' were two different people and so was 'Catherine' and 'Cat'. She stared at the clear Lucite trophy on her shelf surrounded by many other plaques, certificates, and awards. All said 'Catherine' along with her married name.

The person named 'Catherine' seemed so much farther away from who she was now, even more distant than from her then the 'Melle' whose life she had only dreamed about. It was Cat that was beloved amongst the many women who gathered in her shop from every walk of life and it was Catherine who was the respected business owner and suburban Catholic housewife.

As she unloaded her boxes from the van, from the night before, she saw the box of trophies awarded to Catherine the shop owner. She realized that it was time for her to choose who she would be, in this life, now, from that morning on. It had been the first box she filled but the last one she took out of her van as she packed up her store for storage. She grabbed the last box and in Sharpie, marked it 'Catherine', took it out to the garage to put it away, high on a shelf, never to be opened again.

CHAPTER 23

Gabriel Alejandro Couer d'Alene de la Motta d'Dea was a lot of name for a young orphan boy. Usually your name indicated your station in life and, perhaps, at another time, the name would have fit, both him and his station in life. But when his grandmother left him to go back to their monastic settlement where she had made herbal medicines and painted statues of Our Lady, he no longer knew who he was or to whom he belonged.

Despite his new found 'station' in life, he felt, oddly, disconnected from his own popularity within society. 'Abandoned' was how he felt, but his grandmother had not abandoned him as much as he refused to return with her when 'the troubles' began.

"Please, Cucciolo" he remembered how his grandmother had pleaded. "Please. The people are dying! I know how to help them, I have a duty to return, but I have a duty to you too! You are barely a man yet, how can I leave you? Please, please come with me." As guilty as she felt, she knew that his life would be better as a ward of the rich family that was taking him in as their own to educate because he was such a prodigy and also because he had befriended their young daughter whom no one else seemed able to reach.

Their daughter, Aione, had, for a time, lived with her as well to learn how to grow things and to maybe help cure her strange silent behavior. She realized right away that the girl was 'Fae' and didn't need any cure. She needed to be left to her own devices, away from people. Aione must have decided Leandro was not people because they became friends even though they hardly ever talked.

Leandro had never seen his grandmother cry. She had seen and experienced so much in her lifetime that she had decided long ago not to waste her energy on tears or self-pity. Today, however, there were distinct tears in her eyes as she felt her heart, already scarred and broken, break yet again when she held her grandson and her 'adopted' faerie daughter close one last time.

There was no way that a 'wise woman' could remain in the Principality as people were dying everywhere around her and Oublier, as the wanderer Sennische or Jennische peoples were called, seemed impervious to 'La Pest' that left others dead and dying in the streets. She knew she could help. But not here. She would return to Motta. He would stay in Couvet.

Realizing that she would not change his mind she said, "I do not know when I will see you again. I do not know if the sickness may, one day, reach this place." She spoke in a far-off way, already beginning to close her heart to the pain. "For you, I can do this. Take my cures as you have written them down, remember my stories, keep them close and keep them safe. One day, they may save your life. It is all I have left. I will always be with you as long as you do this and remember my songs."

As she hugged him one last time she corrected, "I mean 'Her' songs." and hummed her favorite 'incanto' as she held him one last time. Humming as if planting it somewhere deep inside him. Leandro remembered a scene from his childhood as she rocked him while waiting for the horses to be hitched.

Leandro had been barely twelve when he had carefully transcribed his Grandmother's French written recipes into, both the local German and Latin, along with her 'book of rhymes' that accompanied each mixture. The rhymes were not only 'enchantments', 'incantations' and 'prayers' but they also held secret ingredients that had been withheld from the actual recipes of the potions, tinctures, tisanes and extracts gathered by the women in his family over many generations.

The idea of chanting as a magical practice had not made sense to him at the time but, as he grew older, he began to understand his memories of her singing or humming. As a boy he had no idea that what he had done was heresy and against the laws of the Church.

These precious books were now 'grammaire' because of his Latin and, also, because that was the word that the church used to identify books to be confiscated and/or burned. They were proof that the women who held them were witches, since Latin was a sacred secret language only for men. So, Leandro was left with the books that would have meant sure death for his grandmother.

Leandro had learned Latin at the foot of his 'fathers' who were monks in the fort monastery of Motta d'Dea, devout Catholics who were also Paganis and Sinti Roma 'Aisatta' worshippers or the Black Madonna as the living and literal 'Love of God'.

In the days of his father, studying 'the Lord and the Law' were one and the same. Worshipping 'Lord and Lady' was also the same. Leandro could often be found in the monastery library surrounded by books and scrolls collected from all over the world.

As a young child, he was being raised to become a priest. But that was before the Church in Rome accused the Order of witchcraft and tried to force them to renounce what was called the 'Egypsienne Heresies', namely, the worship of 'Aisata', Black Isis or Black Kali, depending on the sect of monks being accused. Leandro's sect believed both and believed that the 'Heart of the Mother', 'The Love of God' was older than any religion.

"Father, my eyes are sore." Leandro complained after a particularly long study session.

His father smiled as he was preparing clay for more statues. "You've worked hard, I think you need a break. Why don't you go down to the river and see if you can find some of our Mothers?"

It had just rained and waters were flowing down from the melting glaciers. Searching the banks and streams for the little black floating jet shaped like women was a favorite pastime of children after a rain. They were getting more difficult to find, especially when the rains themselves were becoming rare but on a good day, they could gather several and sometimes be rewarded with bits of sweet bread that the monks would make. Leandro, however, knew where floating things would gyre and gather and he could be counted on to find more than most. Today was a good day.

"Look!" Leandro proudly handed his Fathers five small black jet Mothers he had found at his secret whirlpool. They beamed with pride and wonder and gave him a look that filled him so much more than any bits of bread.

"The Mothers favor you" his father said. "You know, Leandro, these were made long ago by the original people here. We are lucky to still find them. They say they represent the Great Mother of All. To them she was a great mother bear." His real father hugged Leandro and gave his mother a secret look of pride.

Leandro smiled as he stuffed the sweet bread in his mouth and watched the monks place one of his little pieces of carved jet inside the Madonna statue at the place of her heart. They left a small hole open where some of the black stone could still be seen. The place, where Leandro thought, that God entered.

The monks then took their own Great Mother pendants that they wore around their neck and rubbed it vigorously against their woolen robes. Reverently, they touched the heart together and watched as a tiny spark flew into the statue. "Couer d'Alene", they whispered. Heart of the Awl. After the spark, he watched as they carefully sealed the hole, hiding the little piece of jet inside and placed the statue on the shelf to dry before firing.

As the years passed, he still believed Gabriel Alejandro Couer d'Alene de Motta Dea was indeed a great name for a young man but it was also a name that linked him to this now forbidden place. In his teens, he realized his name that he shared with his beloved grandmother would be dangerous. So, as he entered adulthood, he decided that he would simply be known as Leandro or Andro Motta. It was, after all, a much more Romanized name and therefore, a safer choice now that the 'troubles' were returning.

Before she left him, his grandmother told him the truth of who his real mother and father was. She left him the Innamorati wagon as his birthright. Also, it was increasingly difficult for her to travel as an 'Oublier', or one of the 'Forgotten' peoples.

The ancient circus wagon that had brought his ancestors all the way from Rome, through France and into Couvet, in Neufchatel, was still with him as he became a young man. After lovingly restoring it, it had followed him to University and, now, back from Basel to Neuchatel the town. It was now where he practiced his grandmother's tea leaf readings for those who knew he had 'the gift'. But to most people, the faded wagon was no more than a fancy lawn ornament in the beautiful gardens of the young magistrate.

Leandro's command of Latin and ability to write in three languages as a child had earned him the patronage of Aldous Henriod, a rich barrister from a wine making family in France, just over the border. Leandro's lighter skin that he inherited from one of his 'fathers', coupled with his dark green hazel eyes, had enabled him to pass as one of the 'locals' and his conversion to a more acceptable form of Catholicism had helped him go to school and study, both, law and the sciences.

The knowledge of plants and animals passed to him from his grandmother, made his studies easy and his knowledge of Canon and Liturgical Law made becoming a barrister even easier. His patron's connections landed him a post in nearby Neufchatel, as it used to be called, and he was able to afford a 'cottage' by the lake where he finally parked his family's wagon that hid three hundred years of a forgotten and secret past.

The young bachelor often entertained with teas and the faded words on his, literally, 'Romantic' wagon, made him a prize highly sought after by the young, rich ladies of the nearby towns. Those faded words, 'Innamorati' or 'The Lovers' could still be seen on what was once a richly painted and ornamented wagon. Women from all over couldn't help but wonder what salacious activities must go on in there.

Leandro, from his studies, knew that these were just stock characters from the old Commedia dell'Arte shows that traveled about Rome but he did nothing to dispel the rumors. After all, it was precisely those same rumors that brought women from all over the neighboring Cantons and beyond to share 'tea' with the rich, handsome and single lawyer.

Only his closest friend knew that he was not 'interested' in becoming 'Innamorati' with them, or any other women. His knowledge of Kabbalah, Tarocchi cards, Tasseomancy or tea reading made him all the more a popular figure in the society of people who could afford to have a second home by the lake.

"Andro!" Aione, his closest childhood friend, rushed to hug him. Aione Argene had traveled with her father, Aldous Henriod, to Neuchatel. Her father had business in the Canton Capital and he had decided to pay a visit to his favorite protégé.

Forgetting protocol, Andro swept Aione into his arms giving her a great bear hug. "Aione! My god, what a surprise!"

Most people referred to her by her middle name Argene, for she was born with a great shock of silver hair and it had stayed the unusual color ever since. But she preferred Aione. Most assumed that she was named for the mountain in the Alps that was said to look like a lion but she knew that she had been named for the Great Mother Bear called Artione by the Paganis, Arduina by the Gauls and, simply 'Alene' by the Helvetian Bear worshippers who were the first inhabitants in these valleys.

She believed the mountains and lakes had souls and that they were her allies. She often said she would draw on their strength, particularly when other children would be cruel to her, as it was not just her hair that made her different.

When they were young, she secretly named herself 'Alene' and Andro became 'Artur' because of his great bear hugs and she still thought of him as Artur but, instead, greeted him by his much more lawyerly name of 'Aleandro'.

He turned to her father, "Monsieur Henriod" Andro bowed slightly, in gracious acknowledgement. "It is a pleasure!" They shook hands then finished with a hug and kiss on both cheeks.

"It has been too long!" Aldous spoke heartily. "We have missed you." This he said with a nod to his daughter, implying that it was in fact she, that did the missing.

Andro ushered them inside and had his staff prepare dinner for his unexpected guests. They spent hours catching up, laughing and sharing memories.

"This has been so good for Argene" her father admitted after she had retired to bed. "Things have not been easy for her. I normally would not bring her on a journey with me but things have been changing at home. People are not so kind to her. She has never been one to play her role well. Her looks alone draw the attention and jealousy of others but then, well, when she speaks…Let's just say she isn't afraid to speak what's on her mind. She has an uncanny way of making people…uncomfortable."

That uncanniness was what drew Andro to her in the first place. He remembered fondly their walks and their talks. As a younger man he entertained the idea of marrying her. Afterall, they did love each other. He knew that. They spoke of it freely.

It was with this in mind that he leaned into her one summer day and gave her a long kiss. He pulled back and looked at her, waiting for her reaction. She responded with one eyebrow raised and said coolly, "Really, Andro?" He was not expecting the reaction he received and remained silent as she continued, "Tell me, did you feel passion?" His surprise turned to annoyance.

"You know I love you".

She laughed. "And I, you. But did you feel passion?"

He became thoughtful. She continued, "Don't you think we deserve passion in our lives as well as love? Excitement, feverish kisses, burning touches…" Looking off to worlds that only she could see, she smiled sadly. "You won't ever feel that with me. I'm not who you want. I am comfortable, I am safe, but I am not Philippe."

Andro's heart dropped into his stomach in a panic. Seeing the look of horror on his face, she continued. "I know all about it, Andro. Don't worry, your secret is safe with me."

She smiled then. It was the kind of smile that let you know that everything would be okay, no matter what.

"How did you know?" he managed to ask after some time.

"I have spies." she laughed and with hands on his hips, his eyebrows furled and his mouth in a 'get serious' pout, he gave her that "look" and playfully punched her on the shoulder.

"Okay, okay!" she laughed again. "Truth be told, the flowers tattled. The Morning Glory flowers. You know their vines connect them everywhere. They creep right up to Philippe's window. They're such children, terrible gossips..." She truly was 'fée'.

They laughed then. Andro knew his secret was indeed safe and he loved her all the more for it. She was the only person around with whom he could be completely himself. The same was true for her. She had learned at a very young age that not everyone saw the world as she did. Not any of her 'worlds'. She learned to, mostly, keep it to herself. It was difficult though. She was sometimes so filled with awe and wonder that she would blurt things out unexpectedly. This would earn her a sharp rebuke as a young child, then gradual isolation as an adult, as her parents chose to keep her away from social events for fear of embarrassment. But instead of protecting her, this reclusive life, coupled with her extreme beauty and her odd knowings only furthered the gossip and stigma that tended to surround her.

When Aione was with him, it was easy for him to slip into one of her worlds right along with her. She was queen of creating realities that always seemed so much better than the one he was in. It was as if she could lose them in some sort of bewitchment in a faraway land from which he always dreaded to return.

While her father was in town consumed by endless meetings and political glad handing, she and Andro escaped to the countryside enjoying long walks and even longer conversations. Sometimes she would remind him of his grandmother. She understood nature around her in a way that only his grandmother did. She could 'see' illness and knew much about the healing arts, albeit in a more abstract and mystical way than even his own family had ever taught him. He understood how she might scare some people but, due to his upbringing, it was, at least for him, a comfort.

It was during one of their walks along the edge of the lake by his home that he spied it. At first, he thought it to be a piece of burnt charcoal floating amongst some dead leaves in the water. The realization, along with the memories, hit him fast and hard. Without thought, he walked into the water, fancy riding boots and all and picked up the jet figurines. Knowing her friend so well, Aione didn't say a word, but watched him from the shore.

The figures were tangled by a leather cord still strung through the holes. He worked to clear the leaves and debris finding them strung together, facing each other forming the shape of a heart. His throat tightened with emotion. He stole a glance skyward as if he expected to actually see his fathers looking down on him.

He untangled the cord and dried it to the best of his ability. Polishing the figures first on his sleeve, he put the pendant on and feeling the familiar spark jump sharply from the figurines to his own heart. From the shore, Aione whispered, "Coeur d'Alene".

CHAPTER 24

The indelible clarity with which Cat was experiencing what happened to Leandro and his father, who was actually his mother, was beginning to invade her waking life. She felt so connected to them but still struggled with the understanding of why this was all happening. Reality seemed less real and she sometimes felt as if she was struggling to keep her life in balance.

The financial pressures, emotional pressures, the legal pressures were overwhelming. She figured either she would emerge from all this as a diamond, or a pile of charcoal dust. There would be no in between. There never seemed to be for her. Her "knowings" came to her in visual flashes and instantaneous understandings. But the understanding of how it all fit, what it all meant to her life now, continued to elude her.

Some of these flashes were terrifying, such as the death of Vanos by the Romans, that she witnessed in the first person. Others were strangely triggered by modern day events such as a conversation with Theo or, as in the case of Max, when she could see some new art he was creating or some sort of alchemical symbols that were coming to him, seemingly from nowhere.

In fact, it was while having tea with that same friend, Max, one day that she experienced one of her 'knowings'. Max was talking about alchemy and Cat asked, "Why were they so obsessed with gold?"

"I'm not so sure it was gold that they were necessarily after. Gold was more of a metaphor. Alchemy would be the process of refining oneself from one's base nature, like a base metal, into a noble nature, or noble metal, like gold. From what I've read, a lot of them were making psychedelics and not so much gold."

"What? Be serious." She hadn't seen them as so altruistic.

"Sure! Think about it, it would open their mind, expand their consciousness. The aim would be to then evolve into a 'higher' form." He said this last as if he were stoned.

"Stop it, Max." she laughed

"How else could they have seen fairies?"

"I've seen fairies and I don't take drugs. I'm perfectly sane!" It was his turn to laughed then.

"Well, mostly." she smiled.

"Okay, okay, to answer your question about your bog ore, sure, I think anything round probably shows it was living at one time."

Cat laughed, "You mean like bog ore being the poop of Piskies…"

Max thought about that, "I guess Pishkie poop is as alive as anything can be."

He went on but her mind could no longer focus on his words. With Max's quip still echoing inside her head, she closed her eyes to better see the images, the knowings, flashing before her.

Aione didn't say a word as Andro walked out of the lake. Instead she wrapped her arms around him and pulled him close. They stood in silence for some time, holding onto each other. Each one knowing that something had changed, something had been set in motion. Each in their own way wished they could hang on forever and not face the ominous unknown that they could feel like the breeze tickling the hairs on the backs of their necks.

"What's burning?" Andro thought as the scent of smoke reached their nostrils and fear hit both of them hard. They ran back across the field to discover what was his once beautiful home, now engulfed in flames. Someone had painted the word 'Nefas' on his door. The word 'Abominentum' was painted on his half-burned carriage house. He and Aione struggled to rescue his horses and wagon but everything else he owned was destroyed.

Andros, still in shock barely heard his dear friends as they pleaded after the fire. "Please, Andro... Please come back home with us." Aione and her father had watched Andro hitch up his horses to the old family wagon. The only things to have survived.

"You are like my son." Aldous spoke gently. "My home is yours."

"Your generosity truly has no bounds, Monsieur" he spoke stiffly in a far-off way, steeling himself to remain resolute. "But there are some things I must do. I have a duty..." His eyes glazed over, lost in memories and they knew they had to let him go.

Leandro headed south without stopping until he found himself at the old monastery fort. He was welcomed there and offered lodging but he chose to live in his wagon the way his family before him had for hundreds of years. He set up just outside of the old garden, long overgrown and started his life over where it began.

It was also near the cave entrance that he knew hid the vast library of the Motta d'Dea. It was rumored that there were books, scrolls and papers from the Great Library of Alexandria hidden there. Also rumored was that it hid the grimoires of many witches who were killed in the first burnings. 'Grammaires' or 'Grimoires' that the Church in Switzerland had sent to Rome to be studied but they 'accidentally' never arrived there having been intercepted by Reformers long ago.

Leandro's own 'grammaires' escaped the fires, being that he had kept them in the little wagon where he always felt closest to his grandmother. It was here at the monastery where he discovered that the two little books, he had transcribed to teach himself Latin and Prussian were just a few of hundreds of books like it that had been collected to study what the monks called 'Alchemy' and the Counter Reformers called witchcraft.

This was not the esoteric nonsense of those who were bilking the church pretending that they could change lead into gold. This was the real alchemy of transmuting one substance into another. The 'craft' was healing, teaching and blessing. The goal was simply to live longer and better and many of these books had been brought here to save the lives of those who were being accused.

The library had not had a keeper in over a hundred years and Leandro found that the brothers there were eager to have someone organize and study the mysterious books that they owned. They had no idea how rare and important they were.

The books were preserved on shelves carved out of white chalk in rooms that were meant to preserve dead bodies but the only corpus they held now were tomes of hand-written books, papers, lead and copper pages, papyrus, scrolls and even tablets of clay and slate. Leandro was impressed to see a printing press here, like the ones he had seen in Zurich and Mainz. He was already theorizing on what local plants could create ink.

But ink would have to wait. Instead, he found himself busy trying to find a better cure for the sickness that was reemerging. The first plague had killed untold thousands and his grandmother was renowned for preventing illness and curing people. Her vinegar and hazel baths were infused with chamomile, lavender and other good smelling flowers but Leandro believed that it was the vinegar that worked. Just as he was sure that salt was also a cure. He already believed that the Orientals had curbed the plague by bathing in salt, sweet, sour, bitter and even meat broths but did not know why that worked. His grandmother theorized that these were all things you do to livestock to stop fleas. Maybe it was fleas that brought the disease.

Leandro had no way of testing this so he began reading the books of wise women who had claimed to have had a cure. After months of study, he had found nothing of substance related specifically to that, but he did find something else that intrigued him.

He found that all witches would only work with 'living food' and that wine, cheese, bread, kefir, yogurts, salted meat like sausages all 'transformed' whatever it was originally into something different and longer lasting. Even immortal.

It also was true that the taste of the food became important as 'elemental' tastes. Like wind to sour or water to salty, they were sometimes described as curing 'humors'. He wasn't sure what that meant but no matter what culture had written the book, they all attributed the success of the process to unseen and unknown beings, forces or energies that must be fed or appeased. It was also important that it was done so in a particular way, element or order. He found himself wishing he could talk to Aione.

It was his own grandmother's book that gave him his first clue. It was not an ingredient but a 'being' that was called to guarantee the success of a potion or unguent. In his grandmother's book she used the word 'lutin' to describe those spirits or beings of the 'hearth'. He had seen other similar mentions. But, instead, words like 'daemon', 'goblins' or 'hobgoblins', were used. Sometimes they would be called 'leprechauns', 'Nain', 'sylphs' and 'homunculus'.

There was no agreement as to what they actually were but there was no mention of 'alchemy' or the 'crafts' of witches that did not have some reliance on these tiny or unseen influences. His grandmother related these beings to the Fates or Fata and she also commended the success of what she did to their queen.

His grandmother, who was known for her 'Oinos Absenthium' cure, relied on a guardian that prevented the mixture from going sour and when she first began creating the wines to increase their potency in the way of the Italians, she still called upon the 'lutin de fée' or the 'fata viridi' who followed Dike or 'Dice' as their queen was called by Latin speakers.

These 'little people' were not generally seen but were invariably called 'green'. Andro remembered also that his Grandmother thought of the age she was born in as 'the Green Age' in the ages of man and that she, Dice, was the harbinger of the Age associated with this new color now gone into hiding, she once said, as man plundered the world for wealth.

Her poems seemed to call them as if they were ancestors who guarded these ways of preserving foods, medicines or drink. As if they were the spirits of a long-gone culture and sometimes referred to Bears and Snakes as a living race. She sang of long-gone Goddesses as if all should know who Dike, Astraea, Asheru and all the others were.

From his Latin studies he knew that the Fée or Fae and the Fata were 'demons' to the church but, here, they seemed like a 'race' onto their own, each having a Queen. And with each loaf of bread, cask of wine or barrel of cheese, they had to be fed an offering from the previous batch to leaven or 'enliven' the mixture. These were used as proof of offerings to Demons.

As an avid gardener, he wished that he could rely on invisible beings to ensure his curatives' success but, as a scientist, he wondered why one person following a recipe would have bad or no results. But, at the same time, he also wondered why his grandmother would mention an ingredient in her songs but those same ingredients were not found in the other books.

These factors were just as good a suspect for failure as not feeding the little people. But the 'little people' and their Queen or Goddess persisted in his studies and he could not shake their existence despite his education. Perhaps that was his Grandmother's influence or maybe Aione, whose voice he often heard when he was getting too far into his skeptical self.

She was well read, herself and said that little people were to be found in every book from ancient Greece, through Rome. There was mention of them, in some form, from all peoples that had gathered in the Cantons to be free. To be educated. Reformation meant they were, therefore, able to write about their beliefs in a common holy language that Leandro understood because so many of them were allowed to learn church Latin before the Counter Reforms.

Aione always spoke of them as connected to the spirits of the plants themselves. She worked with them all the time. He tried to push the thought of her from his mind along with the loneliness that accompanied it. So, Leandro simply put them on the list of 'things unseen' and hoped that he would find some common fact or observation that would explain their presence or mythology.

It was with this thought that he began his garden in the spring. He had been fortunate enough to save the seeds of his last garden as well as to have some seeds from the Dominican Sisters who kept their own large plot just outside the monastery walls.

As he planted, he remembered her famous wine in his grandmother's recipe book and planted all six herbs. She had made an extract with it to cure 'La Pest' and he would often sip the same blend as a tea to cure his stomach ailments as a child. Absently, he began to hum the song he had always heard his grandmother sing when she worked with the plants in her own garden.

Later that evening, cleaned and refreshed from his work in the garden, he settled in to review the incantations from his grandmother's book he had transcribed so long ago. Lost in his thoughts, he began to whisper the words aloud as he read them. As he repeated them a tune came to his mind. He began to hear singing in his head. He hummed along and before he knew it, he was singing aloud. It was the tune his grandmother had always sung coming through the 'incanto', now a voice in his head.

As Cat dreamed through him and listened to him repeat the incantation, she began to hum the tune that her own grandmother used to sing to herself as she made tea for her as a child. The same tune Leandro heard in his head. It was Cat's voice he was hearing; his thoughts had triggered her tune. Was Leandro, in fact, dreaming of her and not the other way around?

Leandro was studying his wine. Some of the monks had asked him to figure out why too many of their casks spoiled in the spring and why some exploded. Leandro was tasting the contents of an exploded cask and was staring at the bubbles rising to the top. He had worked at his patron's winery where they had the same issue and he wondered if he could solve this problem.

Bubbles meant life, he thought. He had considered the bubbles as good but the vintners were intent on making wine taste like it did for a thousand years when made in casks. All winemakers sold their residue to bakers to make the bubbles in bread. Was this the same? His grandmother had made her extracts from the spoiled but free wines, souring some and distilling others. Her famous 'Thieves Vinegar' used an extract of Rue made with distilled wine added to a vinegar to be used as a 'wash', a 'ward' and a 'weirding' agent for divination.

Now he wondered what had made those bubbles 'alive'? Was leavening in bread something alive as well? And finally, was the bolus in a plague patient also filled with something alive? Was it a spirit? Did distilling the wine capture its 'spirit' or did something living give the ability to make men mad and enslave their souls or, in the right hands, make them whole.

Cat was yelling 'Yes!' in her mind as she tried to will Leandro to understand that he was right. However, he could no longer seem to hear her. Perhaps it was just a dream after all. When she awoke, she realized that wise women 'alchemists' were on the verge of learning something really important until the Church banned and stole their knowledge (and them) and tried to bend alchemy to the process of making gold instead of science and medicine.

Ironically, she thought, had the wise women 'alchemists' been allowed to look at living systems like making vinegar, they may have seen that the tiny little balls produced in the waste of soured or bubbly wine was not unlike the little balls that were found in the acidic bogs of Poland that yielded such superior iron. It would have been a short leap to understand how the 'unseen' in the earth could yield the little spheres of gold found in streams all over Switzerland.

Cat saw how close Leandro was to making this discovery but, instead, he decided that he wanted to study the relationship to little people after reading the great alchemist Paracelsus write of 'gnomes, undines, salamanders and sylphs'. He settled on studying the 'liminal spirits' in all things and not the idea of what created living bubbles, good and bad.

It was in his garden that he believed that these creatures aligned with earth, air, fire and water to create the elements for a healing substance. He saw these principles at work in his grandmother's recipes and he saw that she believed that it was singing and rhyming that connected her to them and each other. Aione was always singing to her unseen friends, he recalled. He theorized that these 'spirits' were also akin to house spirits that created diseases but also could give you wine, bread or cures for the plague.

The Swiss Prussians called these 'Kobolds' and they could cause mischief but mainly existed to cause diseases. Those that lived in the wild, though mischievous, were more likely to cause good and went by different names all over the known world like the Cornish Pishkies, Pixies, Tomtes, Knockers, and others. The Kobolds or Kabouters were so called because they were 'Cobalos', a Latin term for 'rogue' elementals that must be driven out, healed or appeased by medicines, foods and even poisons to cure their afflictions that they shared with their human hosts.

The antidote to the black plague, then, was to drive out the elemental spirits that inhabited the stomach that made plague victims vomit, nauseous, have diarrhea and, eventually, turn their skin black or create round 'bubols'. Bubbles. Symptoms that gave the plague its name. Good spirits vs. Bad spirits.

His grandmother knew that elementals and, what she called 'Fatta' of the fae folk, existed but she also knew that diseases were brought to the body by fleas, mice, biting insects and by drinking bad water. Some of the medicines she used had come from her ancestors in India. The Sinti were Hindu and also believed that people needed different body temps to heal (hot, cold, medium) and so needed different foods or medicines. His grandmother knew how to get each from her Absinthe when needed.

When Cat woke up her head was spinning. She had not been asleep long enough to have absorbed all that she was thinking about now but she was afraid that she might forget it and decided to write all of this down in her journal.

Cat wondered if Andro was sipping Champagne what with the bubbles and all. She knew that Henriot was a famous champagne hundreds of years later. She was feeling lightheaded herself. She would have to do some research, however, that would have to wait as a wave of nausea suddenly hit her and she ran for the bathroom...

CHAPTER 25

Oh god, seriously? Now? She couldn't be! The thoughts, the fear, the denial all hit her at once as she stared at the wand in her hand. Standing alone in the bathroom she gripped the sink for stability. The plus sign showing through the little window of the stick in her hand practically screamed at her. "Oh god, oh god, oh god. How am I going to tell Theo?"

She had sometimes fantasized about what it would be like to have a child with him. The thought of sharing a love so deep in a way like that left her emotional. Having ever had those thoughts in the first place left her now wondering if she had actually jinxed herself. It was one thing to fantasize, quite another in reality.

They had five children already, they were struggling financially, barely making it. All of their children were still adjusting to just living together, and now they were to add another? It had been almost eleven years since her last pregnancy. She felt too old to do this again. All of her objections, though, wouldn't change her reality.

She crept back into bed where Theo lay, still sleeping. Keeping as quiet as possible, she lay there next to him, heart pounding, staring at the ceiling.

"Hey" Theo mumbled thick with sleep as he rolled over and draped his arm across her chest. The weight, of not just his arm, began to be too heavy to bear.

"Ted" she shook him a bit. "Are you awake?"

"Mmmhmm"

"No, I mean really awake? I need to talk with you."

"Yeah, I'm awake." this time a little more audibly.

"I took a pregnancy test this morning. It was positive."

Now he was very awake and sat straight up in bed. She looked up at him trying to register if this was good or bad.

"Oh honey, that's great!" he beamed at her.

"What? Really? You think it's great?" She realized he wasn't being sarcastic which brought just enough relief for her to relax. Which meant she had relaxed just enough to no longer be able to hold in her emotions. Once she started crying, she wasn't sure she would be able to stop. The tears came, then the sobs, then the uncontrolled deep cry of everything that she had tried to be brave about for so long.

She wasn't very good at expressing her deepest feelings. She wasn't sure if it was pride, habit or survival that made her hold in all her fears, all the time. But now there was a chink in the wall, and this time, it all crumbled. He held her without saying a word. He just stroked her hair as the tears came in torrents. It wasn't as if she didn't want a baby. In fact, she could think of no greater expression of their love than to have a child.

She thought about how different it felt this time than during her first pregnancies. Then, she wanted the children, but they were for her, not an expression of love. Which made her cry even more.

She worried about how her parents would respond, then thought that was ridiculous as she was a grown ass woman and could do as she pleased. Which made her cry still more.

She also worried about how all their children would respond. More tears. She was terrified about money, about where they would live, about how she would feel as an older mom. Sobs. She was worried about morning sickness, about exhaustion, about work, about getting fat. Then she felt selfish for caring about the petty things. Cried some more. Finally, she was all cried out.

There would be more tears in the days, months and even years to come, but they lessoned as each fear was met. After a time, she began to get excited about this little person growing inside of her. Her mother thought she'd gone mad. Her father kept his thoughts to himself, but she could still feel them through the phone line. Her own daughters had mixed feelings. They would vacillate between excitement and fear. Excitement for a new sibling and fear of what their father would think and say.

It was difficult for them, especially her youngest. If she felt excitement for the new baby, then she felt she would be betraying her father. If she didn't, then it was her mother whom she felt she would betray. Cat let her know she didn't need to feel any particular way. "Just because someone new is joining the family," she said, "doesn't mean you automatically have to love them."

Cat was having an increasingly difficult time with her daughters, they were going through so much. She wanted desperately to be able to make all their pain go away. She wanted to protect them from any kind of hurt at all but knew she couldn't.

Their father was telling them awful things about her that weren't true. But it was her word against his and she was getting tired of defending herself. Her daughters were hurt and confused. They didn't know who to believe or how to make sense of their reality.

She decided to live as openly, as consistently and as full of love as possible. Maybe, hopefully, one day, they would see who she really was and he would no longer be able to confuse them.

Soon, everyone began to refer to the baby as 'Egg'. They didn't know if it was to be a boy of a girl, so 'Egg' seemed to fit. As time went on, the family began to gel more and more. Cat was feeling that this baby was extra special. That somehow, this little egg would be the living connection that bound all the children together. Through him they would truly become a family.

Theo and Cat thought it best that they make their family official. For Cat, they were 'official' the moment she told him they were going to be married. Her heart and her soul, she knew, was bound to his forever and bringing Egg into a single united family was important to them both.

After filling out the necessary paperwork with the city for a marriage license, they had a friend, a minister, stop by one night to sign it and make it official. Surrounded by their children, all crowding around the kitchen counter, Theo and Cat signed the license. There were no speeches, no songs, no rings, just a kiss. It was the most mundane and yet magical thing Cat had ever experienced.

Egg waited till after Easter to be born and Cat decided to name him Alexander Gabriel Henriot-DeMott because 'Egg' was not a good name for a baby boy.

CHAPTER 26

Andro sat alone in his family wagon. He lit his last candle and decided to read. His studies of the books in the monastery allowed him to convince himself that he was doing something other than hiding. The assault on his home and his character triggered more in him than he at first realized. Going back to the place that he thought of as home, he believed would comfort him, would heal him. Instead it left him with more questions. The more he learned, the more he realized he didn't know.

The new Brothers were very kind, but knew little of the violent history of their monastery home. What they had been told, was far different from what Andro knew to be the truth. He was sad and frightened to see history rewritten so soon.

He thought of all those around him who had died as he and his Grandmother kept moving until they finally took refuge at the monastery of Motta d'Dea. Along the way, she had tried to shield him as much as she could but he was quick and smart and not much escaped his eyes or ears.

He could hear the screams and the cries of the families. He could hear the rage in the voices of the townsmen and church leaders. He had watched as his Grandmother tucked away her tools, her books and her talismans when a stranger wandered too close by. He knew that anyone who appeared different, or who held something of value, especially women, would be suspect.

Often, they would disappear. He hoped that they would disappear like he and his Grandmother had. He hoped that they had simply left town, but he knew better. He heard the screams.

Now as he poured over the treasured books of those revered scientists and doctors, he came across a particular passage that when he read it, he felt as if his very breath had been sucked from his soul. What was being called 'medicine' for men was 'witchcraft' for women. Worse, the grammaires proved that men were stealing this from women and saying it was derived 'scientifically'. Now he saw his grandmother's 'Mercurialis' listed as a poison in Paracelsus' writings.

Here it was, as an incomplete recipe, in a book of 'science', masquerading as a curative. The words he used to describe its preparation '...according to the fashion of lay people...' was additional proof to Andro that the sainted Paracelsus, 'Father of Swiss Medicine' was a thief and worse. He was providing evidence of witchcraft to be used by the Church while profiting himself.

With fresh eyes, Andro began scouring the pages of many of these books. He began to recognize more remedies, more incantations as those already known to the 'uneducated', 'illiterate' 'lay' women of many of the villages through which they had travelled.

He had once idolized these great minds from the Universities, now he questioned their research and began to consider them thieves. He began to think of all the books, just here in this monastery, that were hand written, dusty, encoded and somehow familiar.

Instead of seeing books in his mind, he began to see faces, the faces of the women behind the writings, the faces in the fire, the faces of his fathers who once kept the secrets of this place. Who once refused to pass these grammaires on to the Vatican and hid them instead. They who had paid the ultimate price.

He thought of his Grandmother's grammaire. He understood the books could get her in trouble, but he hadn't truly comprehended how much trouble that was. Then the face of his best friend, his Aione, flashed before his eyes and a panic as he had never before felt gripped his heart. He gripped the small jet pendant hidden beneath his shirt and saw a small bear alone in the mountains. He knew he must return to Neuchatel and the Val de Travers.

ABSINTHE, ALEWIVES & ALCHEMY

CHAPTER 27

For days he travelled. The road did him good. The dust that covered him was healing. The smoke from his nightly fires, cleansed him. The stars whispered wisdom and the streams took his tears. He arrived at the estate of his patron, his mentor and his friend feeling stronger, more focused and with a greater sense of purpose than he had ever had before.

The footman who greeted Andro at the gate looked at him in judgement and surprise. Noticing the expression Andro jokingly responded, "I'm sure I'm rather road weary but I wouldn't think I'm so bad as to warrant that reaction!"

"Monsieur, forgive me! I was told to expect your arrival, but I didn't really think..." he drifted off momentarily then more to himself he added, "how could she have known?"

He gathered his wits quickly then passed the horses to the stable boy and ushered Andro inside to rest and to freshen himself. Andro, however, was less concerned about freshness than he was with the well-being of his dearest friends, who were really, the only family he had left. Something had changed here. He could feel it, almost smell it in the atmosphere. It was Death.

"Andro!" Aione rushed into the room. "Thank the Goddess you're here." She looked worn and fragile. He found it hard to believe she could be paler, but her skin had a translucence to it that he had never seen before. Her words tumbled out in a rush, "I knew you would come. I knew you would hear me. Father is ill and he is so anxious to see you."

Andro immediately understood the gravity of the situation. Aione's father was all she had left in the world. Her mother had died years before when Aione was just a young girl. She had grown immensely close to her father. They clung to each other in grief and in joy. He educated her in Latin, French and the new local German. She knew more about the law and politics than most men twice her age. She travelled with him on business, she managed the household and accounting at home. All of this coupled with the medicinal teachings of her mother, who worked with her daily prior to her passing, and at the heels of Andro's Grandmother, left her extremely fascinating, knowledgeable and most undesirable, even dangerous as a potential wife. Her massive dowry and family name did nothing to change the minds of any eligible bachelor within miles. She would be entirely alone and, as a woman, unable to inherit the estate.

Andro quietly entered the darkened bed chamber where he was immediately assaulted by the smell. To his nose, it smelt of bile and death and sweet pot pourri. The heavy drapes blocked not only the light, but any hope of freshness that may have washed through the windows. His ornate mahogany writing desk was covered with papers, untouched and dingy.

He wondered how long Aldous had been in this state? He was cursing himself for not having known sooner. He thought if he had known, he could have helped, he could have used his Grandmother's book, he could have, should have known something to prevent this! Though his guilty conscience didn't respond much to logic, there was the part of him that knew if anything could have been done, Aione would have done it. He knew in his heart she had already tried.

"Ah… My son…" Aldous spoke hoarsely as he turned his head toward the opened door. The words, 'my son', nearly broke Andro and he fell to his knees by his Patron's bedside. The tears fell freely now, yet the words still would not come.

"Aione told me you were on your way. I have been waiting for you." He paused for a few moments to catch his breath as each word took laborious amounts of effort to express.

Andro wanted to tell him to rest his voice. He wanted to tell him everything would be okay, that he would get well. He wanted to make everything alright again. Instead, he stayed silent. He didn't know how much time Aldous had but he knew he would not recover. He would not dishonor or shame this man with lies of good health and delusions. He had too much respect and they had too little time for niceties and platitudes. So instead he waited for Aldous to catch his breath and continue.

"It is important that I speak with you. I am aware of the realities surrounding my daughter. I am aware of what they say. I am aware of the vultures circling my estate." He rested again then before continuing, "Aione will only be a slight annoyance, easily disposed of on their greedy quest for all that I have."

Andro immediately understood where the conversation was headed and he immediately understood what he must do. This family had saved his life, had loved him unconditionally, had given him opportunity, wealth and station. He took a deep breath and finally, he found his voice.

"Monsieur Henriod," he interrupted, straightened himself and formally continued. "I am saddened beyond words to find you in this state. But I am grateful beyond words to have these moments with you. As you know, I have journeyed some great distance and after taking the necessary time to clarify some things in my heart, I have returned. I have returned, Monsieur, if I may, to ask your daughter's hand in marriage."

Aldous looked at Andro then, he saw the young Leandro that he first met all those years ago. He remembered being so impressed with his quick wit, his friendly demeanor, his willingness to please and to learn. He remembered all his kindness shown to his daughter, their laughter and what they thought were private conversations. He knew all about young Leandro then and he knew all about the Andro before him now. It was his business to know. One did not survive in his world by taking unnecessary chances.

He understood immediately the depth of love, duty and commitment that Andro held in his heart that enabled him to make this 'request'. He also knew that as much as this marriage would save the life of his dearest daughter, it too would save the life of this young man whom he already thought of as his son. Aldous smiled then. "All my blessings upon you both."

Cat was feeling particularly sad. She woke with a heaviness on her heart that she just couldn't seem to shake. She hugged all her babies extra hard that day. She felt the need to be near Theo whenever she could. She couldn't say for sure if it was a bit of postpartum depression, exhaustion or the stress of this new unknown reality in her life. Today was another day they would spend in quiet conversation. They had decided to try to figure out how to work from home and create an income that would allow them to both be available to their children.

She was scared. Of course, money was important, but so were her children. She had been taught that success equaled the numbers in the bank account. She had been taught that taking care of someone financially was the most important thing. But was it? She was questioning so many things. Everything she had learned she was supposed to do never matched up with what she felt driven to do.

They decided that they would find a way to be with the children. Theo had left the corporate world, and after a few years in the Black Hills and in Big Sur, California, he was relishing the vindication of having his children returned to him and had no desire to get into the 'rat race' again.

Cat had thought that a store would be the answer but it was only the best metaphor she had at that time. As she continued to change, she realized that she really did not want to sell other people's products or beliefs.

An opportunity to fix up a nineteenth century farm house in town presented an opportunity to have less rent, more space and easy access to the Farmer's market a block away.

After days of talking, they hit upon the idea to capitalize on Theo's skills with flavors and cooking and Cat's skills with herbs and tea making. New Cottage Industry laws that had just been put in place by the new female governor of the state, allowed for them to create teas and spice mixes that they could sell at Farmers Markets and Co-ops without having to work from a licensed kitchen. They ordered jars and labels from a source online as well as wholesale organic herbs and spices.

Their kitchen smelled of amazing and exotic blends and they talked and laughed together as they weighed and packaged their product in the evening after the children were in bed. Terra Stella had morphed into something creative and flavor filled. They both knew it was never about the store, or the stuff. Life seemed to be finally coalescing into something good.

# ABSINTHE, ALEWIVES & ALCHEMY

CHAPTER 28

The wedding of Andro and Aione happened quickly and was supposed to be a small affair but word had spread of Andros' return and he was well loved by many. In addition, there were many who were more than a bit curious about who may have finally captured the heart the 'life-long bachelor'. Those who knew Aione as the odd lone woman who was the daughter of the rich Aldous Henriod, fed the gossip that made people want to be a part of this wedding and Aldous gladly paid to have his daughter become more known and respected by this marriage.

The 'Major' or highest military magistrate of the village, a longtime family friend and Andro's former employer, officiated the ceremony. It was short and carefully devoid of any religious mention but also heartfelt so that people of every religion felt included by the Major's ability to bring people together whether it be a city or a wedding. It didn't hurt that his wife, Magda, was famous for her cooking and knew the importance of a feast.

The mayor also well knew that his town and its ways were being changed by the 'counter-reformations'. He knew that would eventually mean that he, too, would have to resign. He was careful to have Christian witnesses swear this couple's marriage into the books, as he knew what was at stake for the family of Aione. As a military man, it was his habit to look at least three steps ahead and he carefully made sure that his friend's estate and children would be well cared for even in the changing times.

When he had finished the touching ceremony, he nodded to Aione's father and said in Hebrew, 'It is done'. The Catholics in the room echoed him as if he were saying the last words of Christ on the Cross but the Roma, Celts and other 'Paganis' in the room knew what he really meant.

When Andro and Aione stepped out into the sunlight in their first moments as husband and wife, they were met by hundreds cheering from all over, who were friends of the Henriod's and of Andro. Over on the steps of the town hall, however, the newly appointed magistrates of the Canton glared at the old Mayor walking behind the couple.

Their plot had been thwarted. Thwarted by the very man they thought they had driven out of town long ago. Because Andro was a former magistrate and person of standing, there was little they could do to him legally. But legalities were not of much concern to them, there were other ways, like their first attempt to run him out of town. This marriage was merely an annoyance and just a slight delay in their plans.

The new couple celebrated that week but forwent the usual honeymoon despite the fact that they could easily afford the customary year abroad. They both wanted to be near to Aione's ailing father. Andro also had little faith in the new government that was changing things to 'unite' the Swiss and protect against the 'invaders' at their imaginary gates. As a student of history, he had seen this religious nationalism before and Switzerland was surrounded by 'free' states that had Christianized and sent their refuse as refugees into the free Swiss Cantons.

What had happened in Rome, Greece, the Ottomans and the Nordic nations was now happening here and it wouldn't be long before the descendants of those 'refuse' would be blamed for any poverty, natural disasters or diseases that would invariably happen. Already, he had heard of instances of the plague reemerging. Their decision to stay home seemed the safest option all around.

Aione was pleased to stay as well, but for her own reasons. Her hops were near ripe and the women would be coming to help harvest soon. As isolated as she was from regular society and gatherings in town, she had a small circle of women, with whom she met once a month, that she considered her friends. They surprised her now when the newlywed couple finally arrived back at the estate.

"Welcome!" the women shouted in unison but in many languages.

"We hope you're not too tired from this day but we couldn't let it go unmarked by our traditions." The woman who spoke was tall with white hair and tanned leathery skin. Andro noticed she wore a piece of jet about her neck that was similar to the one hanging over his heart.

Aione smiled, a little embarrassed and Andro looked at her questioningly. He recognized some of the women there as being the wives of the city's magistrates. Magda, the old Mayor's wife was present as well as many he did not know. They were such a mixed group of both cultures and status. Andro was curious as to what brought them together here as they would normally never be found socializing in public.

It was Aione's mother who had brought the original group together. Many who were in attendance now were some of those same women and it left Aione with a feeling of comfort, as if her mother was still there with her. It was at their insistence that

Aione had converted their old grape arbors to grow hops ever since their vineyard had been devastated years before due to a blight. A blight that locals thought signaled a return of the plague causing them to abandoned their own vineyards.

Aione used the hops in various medicines that she made. The bitters were an excellent sleep aid among other things. The Major's wife had been teaching Aione and the alewives how to make beer as they did in Belgium, from where she and her Jewish family had been exiled, as well as the beer of her native Poland. When hops were added, the beer would last for months as opposed to only days as was in the case of ale.

The women gathered around the newlyweds cheering and laughing. Some covered them with wreaths and necklaces of flowers while others pushed cups of green opalescent liquid to their lips forcing them to sip the cold, strong anise flavored drink. They wrapped ribbons around their wrists binding them together while singing 'Incantos' in a language that Andro had never heard.

When the flurry of action subsided, the tall aged woman stepped forward. "You have imbibed of the nectar of our kinfolk of this earth. They have agreed to teach you, in Her name." She anointed each of their chests with a rose scented oil. "As your hearts grow together you will walk in love and heal, in Her name."

She dipped her finger then in honey and smeared it across their lips. "You have tasted the sweetness and abundance in life. Now you are tasked to share and bless, in Her name."

She kissed them both on the lips and spoke, "Children of the Great Mother, go now and join as one in the way of our people."

The women all around them cheered and began to encircle them as they pushed them toward the house, and toward their marriage bed.

"Are you okay?" Aione asked Andro after the door had closed.

"I'm not entirely sure what just happened." he felt a bit dizzy, a bit nervous, and more than a bit aroused.

They saw that the room had been filled with scented flowers and a large bear skin was draped over the bed. The singing continued outside. It was accompanied by drumming that seemed to imitate the beat of a heart and ever so slightly, the rhythm would gradually increase in tempo and intensity.

"I'm not ignorant of the purpose of our marriage, Andro" she spoke quietly. "I have no expectations."

When Andro looked at her his heart filled with such love it actually caused him pain.

"Let's not think too much right now." as he couldn't think at all in that moment. He felt conflicted. At the same time, everything seemed strangely clear. Instead he chose to listen to his body. He was often too much caught up in his head, but his body, he knew, would never lie. He stepped closer to her and she smiled.

"I love you Leandro."

"I know." He kissed her lips tasting sweet honey and anise. He pressed his body closer feeling her heat and the smoothness of her skin as her wedding silks slipped to the ground.

He lowered her to the bed, the sensation of the bear fur on her naked back was soft and slightly itchy to her skin. It was momentarily distracting but soon forgotten as his breathing grew heavy, the weight of him pushed against her, and she opened her legs to welcome him. Soon, they were lost in their own rhythms and that of the ever-intensifying sounds of drumming outside.

ABSINTHE, ALEWIVES & ALCHEMY

CHAPTER 29

Andro knew that he needed to become a state recognized scientist and a 'chemist' to legitimize his knowledge and he set about becoming a 'gentleman' using his contacts in Basel to formalize what was a new field of study. He set up his laboratory in the family greenhouse and began growing herbs and spices in earnest and made sure that he was publishing the results. Much of what he was writing was known to him from his days at the monastery. He was just adding the element of the new science to legitimize what his grandmothers and others had always known.

Aione also urged Andro to plant teas for tisanes and she began importing them from wherever she could. She had learned from his grandmother how to dry the herbs without killing them and how to 'enliven' them to heal.

The once shy and strange young woman became quite popular when word got around that she had 'the gift' of tasseomancy or tea leaf reading. Most did not know of her other gifts except the 'alewives' whom she supplied with hops and the mixed group of women who continued to meet with her once a month.

Since she did not need to charge for her 'wisdom' she wasn't disobeying any of the new laws and since their home was on the outside of the town where the family vineyards used to be, they were just out of the reach of the magistrates. Increasingly, many town-women would visit the Henriod Vineyards to drink tea, buy bier and escape the rules of the Counter-Reformers.

The old major and family friend, held on for another year as 'burgermeister' or 'mayoor' but, eventually, he was ousted in favor of someone more in line with the new way of thinking. He had been accused of breaking their Sabbath for missing a Mass when a church Holy Day was placed squarely on one of his 'Juden Feiertag' or Jewish Holidays, forcing him to choose. He chose his own faith, which would have had no consequences a scant two years before. The new laws, however, were becoming increasingly strict and less progressive, the consequences more iron-fisted.

The old major took it in stride and sold his house in town and took up residence near Aione and Andro to be near his old dying friend and to assist Andros in the 'laboratory' taking care of the plants. He was enjoying his late blooming 'green thumb'.

The algae growing on the outside of the earthenware pots that he moved around daily ensured that his thumbs were literally green as he refused to wear the gloves that 'gentleman farmers' usually wore. Having grown up in his own Babciu's garden, he assured Andro he was no 'dandy'. He was, in fact, a 'serious farmer'.

The 'Major' was only ever called by his military rank, 'Herr Mayoor' to the German speakers and 'M. Maire' to the French speakers. He, now, shared his own library and reading room with Andro who called him 'Avus, short for 'Avunculus Corvis' or 'Uncle Crow' for his deep knowledge of astrology and astronomy. Avus' intensive almanack and masonic astronomy charts were a testament to his latent but serious farming skills and his former life as the town historian as well as it's mayor.

His passion was studying the Talmud, Torah, Sephirot and other writings and he was as close to a Rabbi as there legally was. His home often served as a makeshift Synagogue for the remaining Jews in the area. It was also a place where women came to learn how to read from his wife who had been a school teacher when there had been a 'shul' in town. It was a place where all non-Catholic and Christian children could get an education. Many sent their daughters there and many of Magda's former students were now mothers with their own daughters who continued to find any reason to visit the woman whose door was always open.

'Avus' was a tremendous mentor to Andro. The climate down south was quite a bit warmer than in Couvet, which was part of what was called 'The Bear Lands' now split into several Cantons. He found both Avus and Aione invaluable to guide him as to which herbs and plants would do best. Avus understood plants as more than food and, as he could trust Andro more, he revealed that he was called a 'Ba'al Shem' or plant-healer mystic among his own people.

Andro had taken his father in law's name to cement his ownership of the properties outside of the township and he formally shortened his own surname to 'Motta' to remove the reference of goddess worship of his ancestral home. Leandro Henriod-Motta became quite respected by most of the people as an apothecarist and chemist who had such a broad knowledge of cures. His respect only grew as the plague once again began to rear its ugly and deadly head throughout Northeastern Europe.

"Andro, the alewives and I are increasing our production of beer. The water in town has gone bad. The people must have something to drink. We can help them through these times. I am hoping that you will speak to Avus about getting them the supplies. The women in town can make the beer, we won't have to transport it."

"Of course, we will do that right away." Sometimes he wondered why Aione would even care about townsfolk. They were often less than kind to her. But she lived by the charge entrusted to her on their wedding day and as a child of the Great Mother, she would teach, heal and bless in whatever way she could no matter what.

"But this..." she said opening a small book that he had not seen before, "...most requires your help. I will translate for you."

He looked at the strange symbols and what he assumed to be letters of an ancient language. It seemed to be a list of ingredients, a very long list, followed by detailed instructions.

"What is this?"

"You would know it as a Carthusian Elixir"

He gave her a look of surprise. The 'Carthusian Elixir' was a version of the fabled mixture made by monks using a list of 130 ingredients and his grandmother's own 'Extraite d'Absinte'.

"The secret is, well, one of the secrets," she winked, "is that you must not distill the herbs. That will kill their medicine. Instead you must leach and louche. Herbs are alive and must stay that way until they grant us their life and life force."

"I don't understand. You know how to make this. How can I help?"

"Because you're a Doctor." She smiled. "And it's a recipe the Church uses." It was true, Andro was often referred to as a doctor, though he was actually a Doctor of Law, he understood that the people would be willing to accept a medicine from him and the Church would not intercede against a landed gent who was a doctor of law. "The people might be afraid if they knew it was really from me and of course, the Church must not know."

So they worked together as they mixed herbal extracts to take care of this or that sickness, cure the maladies of soldiers and travelers who would often fall ill while traveling to strange places.

Aione was also teaching Andros more about the Lutin. "Your own grandmother used to tell me that the Wormwood family in particular, needs to be appeased if you wish them to work for you. She said to always use enchantment or incantation so that they will give their life and essence voluntarily. My mother taught me that bitter herbs are dangerous unless taken with the permission of the 'fée vert' or green lutin, the fairies. For Absinthe you must appease the Queen of the Fairies."

So they made sure to appease them through songs and musical incantos. At first Andro was simply humoring his wife but he soon saw that her superstitions yielded results. The end result was that they were humming or singing at nearly all times.

While his scientific and skeptical mind laughed at the idea of 'little people' he admitted that even Paracelsus wrote of the 'essential' nature within all herbs and that their 'life' and essence could be restored by adding water and ingesting it. He also wondered sometimes about Aione.

She didn't often speak of her mother. But he assumed it must have been her mother who had taught her so much about these ways. It wasn't her father and, even as a small child and before she met his grandmother, she already knew much. Her knowledge of what had been hidden in the grammaires was impressive considering that she had not read them and, when she played her lute, he often caught snippets of songs he had not heard since his grandmother had left them both as children.

She was so adamant about the little people, he didn't argue with her, instead he accepted the green fairies and tolerated the Major's feeding of them with bits of food and songs from his Jewish mother's people to ward off 'dybbuks' and 'kabouters' that might spoil the herbs or render them useless dead plants. Andro decided that maybe they weren't really 'people' but they were something. Something to be honored and fed with song or sound.

Andro began humming his own grandmother's incantation to the Fata remembering that it was the same song that his 'father' had used when 'quickening' or 'enlivening' the Black Madonna statues that he and his grandmother sold to keep them alive when they originally came to Couvet.

It was in this way that he began to sense that the spirit or heart of his beloved Madonna's were the same 'force' or 'elements' that might fill a cup of tea or a tincture. That is when Andro began searching in earnest for one of those statues that he might have for his own.

Those statues still existed, although many of the little chapels had long since repainted 'Notre Dame' or 'Our Mother' to look more like the local populace. Many had long since lost their ochre plugs and Andro loved that most of the French Speakers in his area still called the pierced heart 'Couer d'Alene' and still called the mother figures 'Santa Aisatta'.

Andro and Aione continued to grow closer, especially now that they were working together and what started out as a marriage 'of convenience', an arrangement between loving friends, became much, much more. It was not long before Aione found that she herself was 'quickening' and expecting their first baby.

She was nervous to tell Andro. A child was never something that they had discussed. Given their arrangement, she wasn't sure how he would react. Of course, she knew how to work with Wormwood and Rue to resolve the dilemma. But she also knew that she wanted to keep this baby and must find the herbs that would ensure that the child would be healthy. She tried to keep it from him for a bit, if only to give her time to work up the courage to tell him but he could read her like he could read his many books and before the day was done, they were discussing names.

Maybe not coincidentally, it was the very next day, while he was out inspecting her vast arbors full of the climbing hops vines, that he discovered an old chapel on the property. When he ventured inside, he discovered a Madonna statue, on a cubit on the altar. Upon inspection, he was thrilled to discover that it was the work of one of his Fathers'.

She had been crudely re-painted to look more like the locals, the scars on her face had been sanded off, but she was undoubtedly from Motta d'Dea. He recognized her motherly expression, clearly one of Motta's trademarks along with the tell-tale hole where the red ochre had since fallen away.

Aione was surprised when Andro returned early. His expression was one of awe and excitement. "Aione, you must come with me! I've discovered something and I have to show you!"

"Now? Really Andro, I'm right in the middle of..." He didn't let her finish but instead grabbed her arm and pulled her outside.

"Come with me!" They walked quickly back across the fields to the edge of their property where the wooded hills began. He led her to a structure tucked within the trees behind the old abandoned grape arbors that had once made the family wine.

He wouldn't tell her what it was. Instead he pulled her up next to him in front of the doors. He took a deep breath then pushed them open dramatically. The low evening sunlight rushed in behind them and flooded the room as they let go of each other's hands.

The light reached the altar and touched the statue upon it. The Madonna radiated back to them in an almost unnatural glow. Aione immediately understood that Andro saw the magic of this place in the same way that she always had. She had shared it with so few and she wept at his excitement.

It was there, as the sun set that Andro finally told Aione his family history. It was also there that Aione decided to tell him a history of her own and that of her little chapel she had, long ago, named 'Notre Dame de la Viridi Fata'.

She pulled a locket from out of her bosom and opened the little silver filigree purse. There, at less than an inch long, was a jet figurine. "It was my mothers. I knew that your grandmother had one as well. I did not know if you believed such things. I know you, sometimes, think my ways are silly but I think she is of the fairies as well. That day at the water when she found you again, I knew that you were for me."

He looked at her and smiled. "I know I am far too learned to deserve you, but I believe in you and 'ergo summa est' I believe what you believe."

"And I believe in you." She turned serious. "Andro, I know that my father has been much concerned for my well-being and what will happen after his death. I know you believe it concerns matters of inheritance and although that's true, there is, well, a little bit more." Aione paused and collected her thoughts. She didn't fear that he wouldn't understand, especially after hearing of his own family's history. Yet she still hoped to phrase it a way that seemed less threatening.

She had long ago learned that any woman who had any perceived power would be in a dangerous position. So much of what she knew and had learned were ways that were only natural to survival but over the years, their intent was perverted and scapegoats were needed. Women were being taught to betray each other, to distrust each other, they were increasingly isolated and reduced to the mere property of men.

"Growing up, my mother had a group of friends, you met some of them." She smiled at the memory of their wedding day. "They would meet here, in this chapel at least once a month. I used to go with her and play outside or sometimes pretend to be asleep in her lap while they talked. These women were all very wise. They were the matriarchs of their families. They would come together to discuss family issues, to share food, help with healings. They would gather flowers and sing songs and they would honor all the mothers that had come before them. Especially the Great Mother, who came before them all." Her eyes wandered to the statue on the altar and her throat felt tight as she tried to hold back tears.

"It wasn't wrong, I swear! It was just something we did! We all did…" She remembered when word got out about her mother and people began to use the word witch. It was then that they began to look at Aione more closely and with critical eyes. Her natural beauty and intuitive ways were perceived to be most unnatural for those in the city.

"We tried to fit in, we tried to go to church, we tried to attend the parties. My mother knew it was important to my father and for his work that we appeared to be like all the others." She took a deep breath then, "But I think because my mother tried so hard, that is what killed her."

"What do you mean?" Aione was almost startled at Andro's question as she had been so lost in her memories.

"She ate their food, she drank their waters. She would never let me partake, but she did. She tried so hard. It made her sick. She never recovered."

"Because she ate their food? Was she poisoned?"

"My mother used to tell me that their food was dead. If you eat death, you become death. My mother's friends all knew. They would share their stock, their starters, their beers. They knew how to make sure their food was alive. The fairies would see how they honored them and would give them their essence. It kept them all strong. It kept their children healthy."

"I'm so sorry Aione."

"I grow the hops for the Alewives, the bees I keep are for the Melissa" Andro wasn't sure what that meant exactly but it seemed vaguely familiar. "Honey is sacred not just to Her, but to all who embody Her."

"Sometimes, not so much anymore, the women still come. We still meet, as you know, but it has never been the same since my mother has gone away.

"Yes, my father is worried about my inheritance. Women owning property is a difficult thing. But a woman who *knows*, things, that's even worse. If I were to have remained unmarried... I'd hate to think what might happen.

"I thank the Goddess every day for you. You have saved my life, in so many ways. You have saved my heart in even more. Perhaps you didn't realize consciously the importance of this chapel, but the magic in you did. It's the same magic that's in me."

CHAPTER 30

Aione's father passed quietly in the night. They had shared a dinner of smoked ham, cheeses, mushrooms and wine all brought up to his stateroom. They celebrated the news of the new baby due in the spring. He had smiled more than he had in such a long time, and although his appetite was still not where it once was, he enjoyed the food almost as much as the company and he spoke of his first grandchild as if he already knew she would be a girl.

As they adjourned for the evening, leaving him to the quiet solitude of his room, Aione looked in on him one last time. She stared at him, memorizing each feature in the dying light as she knew, somewhere deep within, that it would be her last time to do so.

They buried him in the family plot behind the chapel after a rather large funeral in the village church. They were exhausted by the time all was said and done. Aldous had painstakingly transferred all his wealth and property to Andro and Aione as their wedding gift. He did his best to close any loophole and ensure the legally binding transfer could not be questioned or revoked. He knew the vineyards alone were much sought after by many who would seek to profit from their gain, had they known what Aione had done to them. Aione was profiting greatly from all the changes she had made but the town did not, as they lived just outside its boundaries and could not be taxed or tithed. She was a dangerous example for any other woman who might seek to gain independence or sustainability.

Now that the worst had finally come to pass, and Aione no longer had to pretend to be so strong for her father, she seemed to rapidly weaken from the release of all the long-held stress. She was, at the same time, suddenly in demand by the very women who used to avoid her and the new-found popularity also seemed to take its toll. Through it, she still did her best to make all the necessary preparations in the fall for the rapidly approaching winter.

Andro spent less time in his laboratory and more time in his study to be closer to Aione. She tired so easily and was constantly ill. He would bring her cups of raspberry tea and have her suck on anise candies to help with her nausea. As ravenous as she was, she found it difficult to eat and was often in a weakened state. He was at a loss, since none of the things that they did for others seemed to work for her.

For the most part, they had isolated themselves from the news and politics of the town. They were happy to keep to themselves and their studies. It was quite rare now for Andro to venture into the city. He hated to be too far from Aione's side for very long.

Avus took to being their eyes and ears and kept abreast of the latest news through his various contacts still in town. It was Avus who secretly took out a patent in Andro's name to prevent the Reformers from forbidding the sale of the Absinthe as well as the Elixir. It was Avus who warned them of the powers that be who were planning on Annexing their land.

Andro knew enough about the law to know that there was little he would be able to do about it if that was indeed their plan. The new mayor knew that Andro still had many friends in high places and was planning for every potential eventuality when they decided to finally act. Aione had divined this would happen. And it did.

Spring arrived to find the couple anxious and prepared. Andro had worked through the winter to make necessary repairs on the family wagon. He had it stocked with necessities, his grandmother's books and large sums of money that he hid in the secret compartments within its walls.

Aione was anxious for other reasons. The baby growing inside her was quite large now. She was quite uncomfortable. She was so happy that spring had arrived and any warm day would find her wandering slowly to the edge of the property bringing flowers and candles to the small chapel in the woods. The distraction did her good and the walking helped to ease her achy joints.

It was while she was out that the magistrate had arrived, accompanied by two foot soldiers, to deliver the paperwork demanding Andro's land. He responded by throwing it back into their faces and slamming the door. But that wouldn't stop the inevitable. There was not much time left now. He kept the news from Aione for the moment and continued to prepare as best as he could for whatever their future may hold.

Andro had retreated to his beloved greenhouse and began to package up some of his dried herbs and teas for Aione. His hands were shaking with rage at the injustices in his life. In his emotional state he knocked over a jar of dried wormwood and sent it crashing to the ground. The dust rose up to meet him. It left a sweet smell in his nose and a terribly bitter taste in the back of his throat. "How apropos" he thought.

As the dust rose, catching the light, he could swear he momentarily saw a fairy, waving at him as if in distress. It startled him out of his current mindset and he immediately thought of Aione. Aione and her fairies. Aione and her Notre Dame de la Fata Viridi. Aione... he had been so lost in his own thoughts that it didn't occur to him until now that he hadn't seen her since that morning. "Aione!" Dropping his broom, he ran out the door.

Andro ran out of the greenhouse and across the fields headed for their chapel. If she was anywhere, he knew it would be there.

"Aione!" he yelled as he neared the small church. He saw her gathering basket outside the door which stood just a bit ajar. He burst inside to find her on her hands and knees in the middle of a circle of flowers. Her skirt was blood stained, her hair and face shone with sweat.

"Oh god, Aione!" rushing to her side.

"Andro" she could barely speak and was shaking uncontrollably. "My water broke and everything hit so fast. I can't breathe."

"Shhh, it's okay. I'm here, we can do this." He wasn't at all sure that he could but he didn't see how he had much choice. There was no time to fetch the midwife. He helped her get more comfortable and moved some heavy benches closer so that she could push against them with her feet. Then he moved behind her to support her back.

"I'm here" was all he could think of to say, all he could think of to do. It was really up to her now.

"I... have to...push" she barely managed to say through sobs. "Oh god it hurts."

"It'll be okay. It's going to be okay. I swear. Push, go ahead" he was terrified.

She gripped onto his arms that were circled around her chest and followed what her body demanded that she do. She was crying and shaking and more focused than she could ever remember. She felt like she was leaving her body. She felt dizzy and cold but she kept on. After what seemed like hours, her last push brought release and Andro moved around to see his newborn daughter rush into the world.

He wrapped the baby quickly in the shirt he had removed from his body and held her close as his tears cut through his own sweat on his cheeks. Aione collapsed back and smiled. Andro brought the baby to her and lied down beside her. They rested there for some time as the light danced through the windows.

The moment was broken only when they heard shouting in the distance. It was Avus. The urgency in his voice brought Andro to sharp attention and he met him at the Chapel door. "Avus, I'm here!"

"Thank god. Andro, they're at the house. They've brought Gendarmes. They mean to forcibly evict you, annex your lands."

"What are you talking about?" Aione spoke from behind the door.

"Aione, you're here?" Avus stepped past Andro then stopped and gasped. He fell to his knees and whispered, "Aione, my god Aione! The baby!"

"Avus, what are you talking about?" She held her sleeping daughter tightly to her breast as fear stole into her heart.

Andro knelt down beside her, "We knew this was coming, Aione. What I didn't tell you was that they delivered the papers earlier. They don't wish to waste any time. We can't fight them, we have to leave. I have deeded our lands to Avus and they will not be able to use their laws against him. At least for a little while but that will give him time as well as extra time for the women who depend on the hops."

She struggled to process everything. She was too tired, too emotional. She knew that there was talk of them losing her beloved home. Her beloved Chapel. Her beloved 'Alewives'. But somehow, she could never bring herself to accept it. "Now?" she asked incredulously.

"It's not safe for you to go back Andro." Avus interrupted.

"They are already pillaging and looking for any excuse to kill you. They don't want to deal with appeals or fights of any kind."

Aione began to cry.

"You'll be safe here for awhile" Andro tried to soothe her. "I've made preparations." He then turned to Avus, "Dear friend, please, are you able to get to my horses? Can you bring us the wagon? Everything is in there, we are ready to go."

"My boy, it is the very least I can do."

In fact, he had done much more. He and Magda had been planning for this. When the Marshall had arrived, Magda lit two huge haystacks as a signal to the women to gather. They rushed the property and confronted their husbands to cause a distraction as Avus hitched the White Gitane stallions to the wagon.

Avus returned about an hour later. He had raced off with the old family wagon in tow and took a roundabout way to get back to the chapel making sure no one could follow. He had stopped by his home on the way to pick up Magda and some supplies while the steady flow of alewives continued to stall the Vigilante army.

"Oh, my love" Magda spoke gently to Aione upon arrival and quickly got to work. She had the men bring up water from the stream, to which she added oil of lavender and chamomile. She warmed the water as best as she could on the tiny wagon stove. She wished she could make it even warmer, but she didn't dare risk a larger fire, fearing smoke would give them away. She tended to the baby first, cleaning her and wrapping her in new soft blankets.

Then she went to work on Aione. She brought her a tisane of oatstraw, nettle and rose petals and made her eat some dried meats as she cleaned her bruised body. Afterward she helped her into a new dress and made up a soft bed for both new mama and the baby in the back of the old family wagon.

The last thing Aione remembered was staring at the faded painting of the lovers above her bed as the wagon bumped away and her eyes finally succumbed to a fitful sleep. She wasn't sure but she thought she smelled the familiar smell of hops burning and as the wagon rolled past the vineyards, she could hear the voices of many women singing her grandmother's song.

ABSINTHE, ALEWIVES & ALCHEMY

CHAPTER 31

Melle tucked the letter away and prepared herself to speak with her young daughters. It was time they knew. She walked with purpose to her private room at her husband's hotel and opened the hidden panel behind her bed. Light washed in to reveal a small space that contained three books. The books were bound and wrapped in well-worn leather and all were carefully handwritten in both Latin and Prussian.

They were so fragile now, she rarely opened them. Really there was not much need as she had long ago memorized the contents of the pages. She wrapped them carefully in cloth and placed them in the bottom of her market basket along with a small black pendant strung with a leather cord and then headed out to the store.

"Hello my loves." Melle greeted her young daughters with a strained smile as she entered the small shop. Her two eldest daughters were not quite teenagers but loved being grown-up and took their duties seriously. They were usually busy cleaning and organizing up front, her youngest could always be found in the back. This was not an accident.

The family learned early on that the littlest of the three was not one to conform to society. No matter how Melle struggled to teach her the finer points, the girl struggled to edit her comments, wear the proper clothes or even bother with her hair.

Everyone said she was Fae and that poor Melle's youngest babe must have been switched at birth. It was charming when she was younger, but now it only brought sharp rebukes and whispered gossip. It was better to keep her away from the paying customers. But she also had a real gift with the herbs and more often than not, she was found mixing, blending, testing or out in the fields, wildcrafting.

Suzanne was the first to hug her mother. "I thought you were staying home and resting today." She liked to be in charge when her mother wasn't there.

"I told you, she thinks we're too young. We can't be trusted, you know." Charlotte teased.

Melle smiled. "Oh, *you're* not the ones I'm worried about. Is Cécile here?"

"I am!" her youngest daughter came bouncing out of the backroom smiling. She had yellow pollen dust smeared across her nose and tangles in her silver streaked hair.

"Good. You're all together. We must talk" Melle's tone grew more serious and she turned to put the lock on her door so that they would not be disturbed.

"Let's go to the back."

Her daughters followed her with a curious yet somber attitude, even Cécile grew quiet as she immediately intuited the gravity of the situation. They pulled up some chairs and stools and gathered around the tall wooden table that was covered with herbs, pestles and little clay pots.

"Oh, my dear ones, where do I begin?" She took a deep breath and tried to think of the best way to explain their situation.

"Long ago it had come to my attention that our continued success was becoming an increasing thorn in the side of the Major and the vigilantes." she said referring to the men who had been given military rank by the Counter-Reformers.

"What do you mean?" Cécile interrupted.

"Shhhh." her sisters admonished. "Let mother speak!"

"You know, he had tried for years. He and Perrnoud tried to imitate our recipes. He has purchased our supplies, he had tried to pry every bit of information from anyone he supposes may have some, concerning our curatifs." She sighed. "Well it seems that your father had transferred my nostrums, my patents, into your names and said it was to be with your inheritance."

Cécile already knew what she was going to say. Even as Melle said it, the full impact of what this meant had still not hit Melle but Cécile understood. "My great-great-great-grandfather was a chemist and patented the recipe for the Absinthe and the Elixir of Life.

"It was given to me by your tante, your Gran Mere 'Melle' who found the patents in your great ancestor's grammaires and knew that I was his descendant. Your father found it and when I signed over my property to you, my children, I never suspected that he had me do it to own the patents. It had lapsed long ago and he re-registered it in his name using my signature as proof of his ownership.

Your father then sold the recipes to Major DuBier when you were just babies and the Major is now claiming that Dr. Ordinaire really invented it. He had already opened a distillery with Perrenoud's son. And now your father is backing the younger Perronoud in his own distillery."

Cécile's face was beginning to turn red with anger. "But Dr. Ordinaire is a fraud… And father is a…" She tried to contain her real thoughts. There was worse she could say about the Dr. But the worst was her feelings of betrayal by her father. Not that she had ever shared them with anyone, but even as an eight-year-old, she knew that she would be the next 'Melisande'. She took it very hard when the original Melle passed over to the other side, but she still talked to her 'Gran Mere Melisande' when she was alone.

Even at eight, she would often venture through the countryside trading medicines for herbs and recipes. She was loved by the people outside of the city and she loved their ways and teachings. She thought she could be of an even greater success if she could share them through the store. Then the people here would finally love her too.

She didn't realize that her mother had been doing just that but it had only brought her resentment, not love. She knew that the 'Major', a lace maker who forced women to make lace for his own profit, had been trying to do the same with curatifs made by women. He was already trying to get apothecary laws passed in the village. Now her father had joined them.

"His creations will never be as good as ours. He doesn't understand that what he creates is dead. He does not honor the spirit within the herbs, he does not ask for their permission…" She stopped herself from going on.

She wanted to say that she knew about their lottery, their embezzlements and even why he never slept with her mother. She stopped herself but mother and daughter had a connection that didn't heed or need words. Melle just nodded her acknowledgement.

"Mother, I'm sorry, I don't understand. Are you saying that we cannot make Absinthe?" Charlotte asked, thinking about money.

"Not anymore." Melle was being brave but there was no way she could change it. "The Major stopped by and informed me that I was to cease and desist. That Absinthe was no longer a Nostrum, a patent medicine, and only he could produce it as a 'curatif', as medicine." But Melle already knew that her husband was double crossing Dubier and that he intends to make it in France with the young Perronoud so that he can sell it legally as an aperitif and escape the law."

"But surely the major doesn't have the real recipe. Wouldn't he have been making it?" Suzanne interjected defiantly.

"Your father sold the ingredients but the process was hidden in my grammaires. A recipe means something different than you think." She reached into her basket and pulled out the wrapped cloth. "They can cheat each other, steal or do what they want. They only have a list. That is why they are stopping us by other means."

She carefully unwrapped the bundle. "My dear ones, it's time you know where you came from. There are some things that are more important than money. More important than business or titles."

She placed the cloth on her lap revealing the books for the first time. "They will make something of the ingredients. But it will not be Absinthe. I will not let them know any more."

She was looking at young Cécile, who was really the only one who understood already what she was saying. "Our family has a long history of knowing how to work with nature. We have long been able to survive, even the darkest of times, because we were gifted with knowledge that we have been able to keep alive through the centuries.

"These books contain all that knowledge. They were passed to me after I became the Melisande. I was told they once belonged to my great-great-great grandmother Aione Henriod-Motta. She was said to have been a fairy princess, her mother, a Queen of the Fae." She smiled at the retelling.

"The book was only to be handed down to the women of the family trusted enough to protect our secrets. And now I have been blessed with beautiful daughters! I will entrust these secrets to you." Her daughters all grew quiet and anxiously waited for her to continue.

She grew serious. "Our family, also, has a history of not fitting in with Society. I've taught you all much of what I know, and there is even more in here. It will serve you. It will keep you alive and I mean that quite literally." She looked at them sharply, her two older girls wincing at the thought of 'surviving'.

"But what you must understand is that for some, knowledge is power, for others, it is a death sentence. There is too much unrest these days. Sometimes it is better to walk away and fight another day."

Suzanne was angry. She had just seen her life of privilege and luxury disappear. "What does that even mean? Why can't father buy it back?"

"Your father sold it to the Major because he knew that it would be considered witchcraft for a woman to own a medicine that is no longer a nostrum. My father was a judge and your father is a lieutenant. They are vigilante. He bought the hotel with your birthright. The sale of the nostrum helped finance that."

"What's that?" Cécile spoke up first, noticing the pendant peeking out from beneath the books.

"A 'nostrum' is a patent. It really means that the Church Government owns the recipe and that we have a license to make it. Had a license…"

"No. I mean, what is that hanging on the books?"

"Oh. That is Our Lady in her earliest form. These were carved by the Bear people long before Man's religion and it was worn by the women. It is said that the women were buried on the shores of the great lakes and in the glaciers, sometimes, when it rains, their bodies wash into the lake and these float up."

Cécile mouthed the words, "Nostra Damus." Then she looked at the books. She looked at her mother. "Nostrum."

"Yes, this" Melle smiled "This is our Mother." she tugged on the fine but old braided leather to reveal the carved black piece of jet. "This reminds us to never forget from where it is we come, to always remember to whom it is, that we belong."

"It's just like mine" Cécile said quietly and she tugged her own leather cord about her neck to reveal her own little piece of jet that she wore over her heart.

Melle's eyes grew wide. "Where did you get that?"

"I found it floating in the lake. She told me to keep Her close."

"Who told you?"

"She did." Cécile held up her pendant. "Her." She turned the little black figure to face her as if it were talking even now.

Melle grew quiet, thoughtful, her eyes brimmed with tears that she refused to allow to spill. Swallowing hard, she changed the subject.

"I'm so sorry my loves, we will be closing. Effective immediately."

"What? We can't!" Cécile cried.

"We don't have a choice. We are far too bold as it is. Major Dubied is far too connected. The town, the church, the Prussians, all stand behind him. We cannot cross him. Your father…"

She paused to try to hold back her tears and her outburst that would say too much. "Your father has signed on to this letter confirming that we are to stop making Absinthe or Elixir. We cannot run a store selling only candles and tea."

She bit her lip to contain her mounting anger. "He sold the recipes in order to save the hotel and to stop us from being accused of witchcraft." She knew that this was only partly true.

"It's not fair!" Cécile ran out the back door slamming it behind her. Charlotte stood to go after her.

"Let her go." Melle said quietly.

Melle had been so wrapped up in her own guilt and desires for independence that she hadn't fully realized the depth of the magic within her youngest child. She knew there was nothing that she could say to make it better.

Suzanne interrupted. "So, are we poor?" Charlotte knew better than to interrupt her mother when she was angry but she was wondering the same. Their father had not done well with his money and Charlotte had already wondered how much the books were worth.

Melle just looked at them sadly and bit off her words sharply. "You will never hunger. You will never thirst." She wrapped the books back up and walked briskly to the door to see if she could see Cécile.

Cécile continued running blindly until she was far out of town. She finally collapsed out of breath in the middle of a field. She stared at a large honey bee circling a hyssop flower in front of her as she caught her breath and she squeezed the little jet figure in her hand tightly. She began pulling up the plants to create a circle about her. She pulled up some hyssop and swept the area clean. She plopped down in the middle and cried but only for a moment.

A feeling of resolve washed over her. Still angry, she dried her tears and looked about. She spied some mint. "Perfect" she thought. As she picked some, she noticed the Chamomile growing nearby. "Yes." She grabbed that too.

Cécile flopped back down in the middle of her circle, arranged the mint into a little pile and placed her pendant on the top. Then she closed her eyes.

"Grand-mere, help me. You know my heart. How can I stop this? How can I make it all go away? I am not my sisters. It is not the money. Our father did not have the right..." She was tempted to cry again but decided she needed to be brave and prove that she was ready to be a true daughter of the Melissa. The large honey bee landed on the necklace as if in response and began to explore the mint. Cécile stared at it thoughtfully.

'Sometimes it is better to fight another day' They were the words of her own Mother, but they seemed to be more than that too. She heard her Grand-mere's gentle voice in the buzzing, saw her and many more looking back from seemingly a thousand tiny eyes.

"I don't want to fight another day, I want to fight now!"

This time the voice spoke inside her. It was still gentle but commanding, 'You still have much to learn. You must only do what you can. Your time will come my little one. This is still the Time of Man.' This was not a voice she was about to argue with though she didn't much care for the message.

She took a deep breath, closed her eyes one more time. She envisioned the circle around her, she felt safe within its boundaries. She calmed her mind and slowed her pounding heart.

When she opened her eyes again it seemed she was viewing the world around her through a bubble. The sky, the field, the flowers all seemed to be sparkling, their colors were more intense and they seemed to be alive. They would move, not with the breeze but in their own kind of dance. She saw little lights, that were not of the sun, flitting amongst the tall grasses. When she spoke, even her own voice seemed to come from outside of her.

"With my all of my heart, all of my mind and all of my soul, I will keep your secrets until such a time that they will be safe to give to the world. I promise you, my Great Mother, that I will return. For my mothers, for my daughters, for myself, I will teach in Your name, heal in Your name and bless in Your name. For now, and for always." She placed the chamomile blossoms on top of the pendant and whispered, "Por Justitia."

Chapter 32

Cat's dreamstates whipped her back and forth in time and she was finding it difficult to keep it all together, especially when she might envision two different lives and times in a single night. But she was putting it together that Andro had been the one to 'patent' the Absinthe ingredients but he had neglected to patent the process or the enchantment. A patent would have protected Aione's ability to sell curatives without a doctor involved. Sort of like an over the counter medicine.

She pieced together more when she dreamed about their escape from Couvet to return back to the place where he grew up as a child. She saw in her dream the little wagon leaving in the opposite direction of Motta d'Dea but soon realized why.

Andro and Aione would arrive at the monastery of his father in a trip that took several days. But he had first gone East and North to Monruz to visit the Benedictines there knowing that they would give the family a place to stay in exchange for Absinthe and 'Elixir of Life'. While this was in the opposite direction it was the only way that a wagon could traverse as the valley of Neuchatel led to the valley of Lausanne, a sister lake that shared a valley in the mountains. A dispute with the Carthusians had cut off the Benedictines' supply and the monks had come to him some months before having heard that he had also unlocked 'The List' that was the only clue to the ancient elixir stolen in the Siege of Savoy by the French long ago. But Andro had the original list and knew from his Absinthe process what to do with that knowledge.

Father Georges greeted them warmly and when they told him of their plight, he offered the monastery as their permanent refuge.

"Bless you, Father but I don't think that you want to harbor witches." He half laughed but it was more than half true.

"My son, we are all witches in the eyes of the New Church." He lowered his voice and leaned in to continue. "Did you know that they are even considering our blessed Hildegard as a witch?"

He was referring to Hildegarde Von Bingen the Benedictine Abbess and Alchemist whose music he had heard in Basel at the University. The University where he met the young seminarian now known to him as Father Georges. One of the reasons that Father Georges was a devotee of Absinthe was that Hildegarde extolled the virtues of Fennel and Anise, along with honey, as having given her the power to 'see' hundreds of years before.

The Benedictine monk was thrilled to have some Elixir d'Vie delivered to him and even more happy to have some Absinthe as the wasting sickness and rumors of the plague were coming north.

"I have heard many good things about your Absinthe, Lady Aione. One more miracle and the Holy Father would have to put you up for sainthood."

Aione bowed low and smiled. "Your Holy Father would do well to tell your Prussian prince what happens when you kill all the healing women."

Father Georges kissed her hand gallantly and took her arm. "Let's leave this old dullard to unload the luggage and let me take a look at that baby, my lady." Andro bowed mockingly low as they passed by and Aione winked at him adding, "I will have tea in the confessional, thank you…"

Andro laughed. "I will be awhile, m'lady, but I'm sure you'll probably still be there confessing long after I'm done."

Andro unloaded several cases of the elixir and a case of Absinthe and several novices and monks joined to help unload the heavy jars. Andro was pleased to see that there were nuns here now and very pleased to hear them singing Mother Von Bingen's music in the echoing church sanctuary. He knew that Father Georges was in charge of teaching music but had never heard Von Bingen actually sung by nuns.

"Your novices sound lovely." Andro said as they left the Sanctuary Narthax where the sound of the nuns' music filled the ceilings and echoed for several seconds. "How did you teach them?"

Father Georges laughed "I find women superior to men when it comes to learning anything."

"Touché … I meant is there some sort of notation you use to mark the melodies?"

"Oh, yes. Mother Abbess Von Bingen had created her own notation that makes it easy to mark the melody as well as harmonies and the all-important timing."

Andro smiled. "Do you suppose a man could learn it?"

Father Georges laughed. "Perhaps, if he were not as old as, say, yourself. Any particular reason?"

Andro got serious. "I am told that the Blackness is returning and I would like to sing and teach the incantations that go with the elixirs." He looked at Father Georges to see his reaction.

Father Georges also turned serious. "I think that's a good idea, we had better do that; and don't think that I don't know you feed the Lutin with song." He added using the French word for fairies. "Avus told me. The old crow also told me that your singing has not improved since our school days but I will write the incantations down if your good lady will sing them for me. I will also gift you with one of our primers with which we teach the notations. It was printed for us on our very own Gutenberg." Andro was impressed and asked to see their machine and then he went to get Aione and the baby.

The couple ended up staying a few more days than they had expected. The father told them that the monks in Motta d'Dea had been driven out by the Swiss Church that was expanding its power everywhere. The Dominicans quickly moved in and declared it a Sanctuary before the Reformers or the Archbishop in Geneve began to nose around. Andro knew the Dominican Abbess there when she was just a nun. He knew she would guard the secrets and take good care of the gardens.

Father Georges sent word ahead that they were coming and they would leave as soon as they brought back word that it was safe.

They had a good time teaching the incantations and father Georges decided that he would label them as 'enchanting lute melodies of the year' which was a play on words of the lake near Motta d'Dea and a clue to where the cave of the Lutin Queen might be found.

Aione played her lute and quickly picked up the notation. She was eager to begin notating the rest of the book of incantations as well as to learn new ones. But she still needed to heal since having given birth and now that her milk was coming in, she hoped that both she and the baby would be getting stronger soon.

Father Georges gave Aione beer to take on their journey to help her with nursing. He assured them there would be plenty more at Motta d'Dea. The Dominicans were famous for their bier and their fresh ale in the Springtime. Aione had never been to the place of her married name but she already loved it as well as the nuns who dwelt there.

The messenger returned after two more days' time with news that it was safe to travel. They left with fresh new French Gitane horses and a mule to carry gifts, the bier and extra belongings, which gave them a little more room in the wagon.

The nuns were sad to see the baby go. So sad, in fact, Aione was beginning to wonder if they were going to kidnap her baby, they loved her so much and when they learned that she still had no name, the novices begged her to ask the Abbess to do the honors.

The morning before they left, Father George baptized the little girl and the Abbess chanted for a vision. After quite some time, the Abbess suddenly fainted right next to the baptismal font. After she was awakened with the Holy Water she smiled and asked to hold the child. Aione sat down next to her while a novice helped her swaddle the little girl to place in her arms.

"Little maiden, I dreamt that I was in a vast cave. A cave so old that it had been there long before these lands had names and borders. Long before men ruled. It had been there long before the lake, which sits at its feet, was born. It was there when the people who carved the little jet grandmothers were the only ones here.

"In that cave, you were brought before the Great Mother and you were baptized in a font whose water rushed forth from the cave floor. You are to be named after that holy fountain to which you have returned in this lifetime. You are marked, Child, and do not belong, like other children, to the Mother. You are a child of the Grand Mothers and you are the first of many to return.

You shall be called after the 'La Vie Eau', The Water of Life. We shall know you as LaVieauna, 'Little One of the Sacred Waters'."

The Abbess prayed with Aione and sang a song to the baby of the Bear people. As they were leaving, she gave Andro a little cloth bag full of jet figures that her novices had collected whenever they floated up on the shore of the great lake. Andro took one and rubbed it on his sleeve and sparked it to his own. "Couer d'Alene." He whispered and returned it to the Abbess.

CHAPTER 33

It took several days to reach Motta d'Dea. Aione required a lot of rest which was not possible when the wagon was moving. All along the way, people with all of their belongings, were walking in the opposite direction. Andro learned what people were calling 'the plague' had returned. Some travelers were fleeing the Black Death, still others were fleeing authorities who were blaming the outbreak on witchcraft. Andro learned that the 'Ethanikos' or Heathens were being accused of poisoning the waters.

After hearing the unsettling news, they considered whether it would be wise to continue. Aione decided it would be best to divine on it. She pulled out a small wooden plate, on it was painted hexagonal designs that looked like a beehive. She held a single 'dice' cube and asked the board questions as she dropped the die on the board.

"The plague has indeed returned and we must go to your home in the mountains and do what we can. They will need Absinthe and even, perhaps, the Elixir of Life." Andro nodded and hitched up the horses that had been grazing.

The nuns had been expecting their arrival and greeted them warmly. Aione was pleased to learn that the nuns here also sang although from a different canon then the Benedictines. Andro was pleased to know that his garden was still intact and that the nuns had converted the fallow vineyards to hops just as Aione had done. He was most pleased to see that the nuns had restored the kilns and they were, once again, making the Madonna figures for which the fort had been previously known.

He gave the little jet figurines to the Abbess who had been taught by the monks how to use them. She crossed herself and thanked him by mouthing the words 'Coeur d'Alene.'

They parked their wagon by the overgrown pad that used to be on the edge of the garden. It was now surrounded on all sides by the garden that the nuns had created by carrying black soil from he knew not where. He reached down to inspect it. It smelled smoky, it was loamy and deep. It was filled with a fine silky matting he had only seen once before.

The Abbess noted his appreciation as he brought a sample back to the wagon for Aione to smell. "You have discovered our secret."

Andro smiled. "I was about to say that you discovered ours. I have only seen soil like this in the north of where we lived."

The Abbess smiled. "Come with me." She walked to the cave entrance that had once been Andro's office. Once inside, he noticed that they had added to the already large library. There were many nuns and novices reading here now, whereas before he had been the only one. He saw that they were transcribing and translating from Latin by torchlight.

"Our sisters are transcribing our craft from the Latin as this makes learning still a heresy here. Even for us sisters." She continued to walk past them and he followed.

They walked past the catacombs were the skulls and skeletons of martyrs were neatly stacked on limestone shelves which had been carved deep into the smooth walls. Andro noticed that the great wooden bookshelf at the end of the long catacomb that once held the most precious scrolls and papyrus was no longer there. Instead there was an opening where the tunnel seemed to continue.

He looked down at his feet and noted that the simple chalk floor gave way to tiles that became more and more intricate.

"Who built this?"

"We do not know. We found it like this."

The tunnel lead to a large room that seemed to shine as the walls were polished and marblelike. He saw that the large room was designed in a hexagonal shape with a doorway in six directions. He looked at the floor and saw that it was made up of more hexagonal tiles that looked exactly like Aione's divination board. Even down to the bees that were inlaid along with the different flowers in which they appeared to be flying.

As their torch light reached the first wall, he saw that it was inscribed with symbols he could not recognize. Each wall had similar inscriptions carved in them, but in different forms of symbols. Andro intuited that they all said the same thing.

In the center of the room he saw something familiar. It was a large stone cube that he recognized from his own chapel in Couvet. Aione called it a 'cubit' and said that her little 'die' in her divination board was a 'cubit' as well. Andro had always thought of a 'cubit' as the measurement of a forearm in length and the cube was approximately that size in every direction.

He looked at the well-worn cube and saw that at one time it had been carved with sigils now too worn and faded to see but he assumed though that they matched his wife's painted cubit at home. He knew she would be thrilled to see this and he couldn't wait to show her.

"There is more to see." The Abbess motioned to the door opposite the one through which they had entered. Here there was a much, much larger room, a natural cavern with a ceiling higher than any cathedral ceiling he had ever seen. Large stalagmites and stalactite spires surrounded a small pool in the center that had well worn stones laid in a rough circle around it.

The Abbess watched him as he carefully walked to its edge. "She is our Oracle, 'Aquae Vitae'. The Grand Mothers without name speak through her. The Ones from the Stars."

Andro approached the well reverently and the waters seemed to glow with a yellow green opalescence that reminded him of how Absinthe and the Elixir of Life seemed to glow with the addition of water. "Aquae Vitae" he repeated to himself. "La Vie Eau."

The Abbess left him there and continued to move purposefully forward toward the daylight streaming in from the South. Andro broke his reverie and followed her and as he ducked down in the low cave entrance, he placed his hand in a small stone depression filled with water and crossed himself. When he stood straight up again to exit the cave, he saw, in the distance, the sun reflecting on a large beautiful lake surrounded by a valley of impossible green. Nuns were filling sacks of black loam beneath him and he knew that this was the place that the Abbess had divined.

He was home.

CHAPTER 34

Melle, the younger, never recovered from the loss of her legacy and birthright that had been passed and entrusted to her. Cat no longer saw her in dreams but only through the sad memories of Cécile who had left Couvet and had returned to Motta.

She had thought to become a nun but when she arrived, she soon realized that she had neither the temperament nor the attention span to be an initiate. Not to mention that being a 'bride of Christ' insinuated that she loved Christ and that could not be further from the truth.

She did find herself useful, however, as the sisters knew that she was the daughter of Melle and her family's Absinthe was still treasured and remembered here. In fact, it was still remembered in all the nearby areas where the Plague had repeatedly tried to rear its ugly head over the many years but was repelled by the 'Fatta Viridi' and her green elixir.

The sisters looked at Melle's frail and wispy daughter and smiled at her flighty and cheerful ways. They had doubts about whether she could produce the elixir but once allowed into her great-great-grandfather's apothecary lab, the doubts dissipated quickly. She not only produced the elixir of the fairies but she also concocted her own version of the 'Elixir of Life'. She used the herbs available locally and learned how to imitate the ones found only in rare, exotic and expensive ways.

They called her new Elixir 'Chantreuse' because of the way Cécile sang over every batch. She also sang as she administered every spoonful to her steadily growing stream of patients who came to see the one the sisters called the 'Sacred Oddling'.

The local 'Oublier' adopted her as one of their own. She soon became a part of their 'hive'. She was not very good socially but she became the oracle when it was discovered that she had a gift for the 'board and cubit', the divination that all 'hives' used no matter their religion or culture.

Most used a simple plate and Roman gambling die but Cécile had the delicately decorated hive version that her mother had passed down to her. Over time, she became the 'Mellissa' or as they called her here 'Melona' or 'Melania' depending on whether the speaker was French or Italian. In the rural areas surrounding the caves she was treated like rare but delicate royalty and the people made sure that her needs were met. For the most part, she was left alone unless someone was sick or troubled.

She lived in the garden of the sisters in the tiny wagon that had been placed there so long ago it had become part of the landscape, buried in vines, roots and brambles that had entwined its wheels as if to make sure that she would never wander again.

Not one to be tied down, she ably restored the old wagon, freeing it from its earthly bonds and making it wander-worthy once more. Her many friends and patients recreated and replaced the wood and iron long since rotted and rusted and even the children helped hand sand every inch of the ancient relic. She, then, lovingly restored the paintings and carefully recreated the 'Innamorati' scenes inside.

She lived in it but she could also be seen taking it to the markets and driving it with her two white horses into villages that needed her help.

Cat realized while watching her paint that Cecile had the same eclectic way of holding her brushes as well as her use of colors. She dreamed of her frequently and she often felt like she, herself, was one of her fairies that followed her in the garden. She watched her preparing the elixirs and advising people wisely as a personal oracle. She also watched her in the cave whenever the Hives or 'Hohenwald', as the Reformers had named them long ago, were called together to celebrate the turns of the year or, sometimes, when a problem needed to be dealt with by the people of the countryside.

Cat realized that every dream seemed to be a reflection of something in her own real life. That is why she was especially upset to dream of her when she was administering to a Roman soldier from nearby Geneve.

The Byzantine sisters had found him as they were going to celebrate the Solstice with the other hives. He was lying, semi-conscious, on the side of the road apparently injured. It was highly irregular to allow a soldier inside the walls of their compound, as this was a sanctuary but he was not moving and his groans convinced them that the best thing to do would be to take him to 'The Melissa', as they still called her, for healing.

They laid him on the floor of her wagon as was customary then left to find her. Cécile was tending to the herbs that she grew on the long hops vines when the Sisters approached.

"Cécile! We have found a soldier in need of tending. We have seen no wound but he groans so, obviously in pain. We hope that you may be able to ascertain his illness. Perhaps you can help him?"

"A soldier?"

"He's not vigilante. He looks to be a member of the cantonal troop, maybe Lausanne. We've no idea why he may have wandered out here."

"Perhaps delirium?" another Sister added.

"Very well then, I shall see to him."

Cécile felt the hairs on the top of her head stand on end and a tingling sensation reached across her scalp. She stood still for a moment to ascertain its meaning. She listened for more information, as usually when she felt this, it meant that someone or something was trying to warn her. But nothing else came to her so she proceeded to make her way back to her wagon and was left alone to look at her patient.

She entered quietly and took note of the man lying on the floor. He was seemingly unconscious. His eyes were closed and he was very still, but for his breathing. She noticed that was rather heavy, labored? She thought she recognized him from the spice market in Lausanne. The space was tight in the wagon and she stepped carefully to the bed and reached for her divination board to see if she could divine what it was exactly that she was dealing with. The moment she laid her hand on its honeycomb design, she knew. Spinning wildly, she took in a sharp breath.

"You are not sick." It was not a question.

Her mind was still trying to process the sudden knowing as he leapt up from the floor and pinned her to the bed. She tried to scream but he covered her mouth with his hand. "Silenzio, puttana!" He had called her a whore. That was all she remembered.

No one thought anything of it as they saw him leave later and walk calmly out of the gates of the sanctuary. No one heard Cécile quietly crying alone in the wagon. She curled up tightly to make herself as small as possible and closed her eyes against the pain and the shame.

She left the little wagon to care for herself only once it was long past dark and after everyone had gone to bed. Cat had witnessed the whole thing as she had experienced it through Cécile. And she too lay weeping in her bed just as if it had happened to her. It had.

Cécile's first thought was to thank the goddess that she was too old to bear a baby. Cat knew, from experience, that this was not true. And, really, so did Cécile. It wasn't too much later that her worst fears were realized and Cécile found herself with child.

Although she knew that Wormwood and Rue could be taken to prevent this life, she couldn't bring herself to take them. Something unimaginably horrible had already happened and she decided that she would do whatever was in her power to turn it into something good.

The baby born to Cécile was a girl. She decided to name her 'Aikaterina'. Aikaterina meant 'pure', because she would be pure in spite of her birth. And because of her birth, she, Hecaterina, in her language, would be dedicated to 'Hecat' and would know no Roman God. Only magic.

ABSINTHE, ALEWIVES & ALCHEMY

CHAPTER 35

Cat and Theo continued to have growing success with their teas and spices. They were being urged to market their most popular blends on a larger scale. To enter into a bigger market however meant different regulations and more investment. They worked out the math and made a plan to have enough saved to make the leap within a year.

During this time, Cat was surprised to feel that familiar nausea in the mornings. A quick test confirmed her suspicion. She was once again with child.

"I don't understand, we've been so careful!" she lamented.

"It'll be okay" Theo assured her that, in his priestly world, "A baby is a blessing!" Easy to say when you aren't the actual bearer of this little blessing.

It took a few weeks for everyone to adjust to the news, but before long everyone was excited. Because she was an older mom, her doctor had scheduled her for an ultrasound. Theo and their three daughters went to the appointment with her. All were eager to see the new baby. It became clear however, after only a few moments in, that something was wrong. The technician left the room almost immediately to get the doctor. After a few more quiet moments of the two of them reviewing the pictures on the screen, they spoke.

"We're so sorry, they began. "But we're not finding a heartbeat."

Cat already knew before the technician had first left the room but hoped that her intuition was wrong. She felt all the air leave her lungs when the worst was confirmed but she did her best to keep the sadness from heart in that moment, trying to be strong for her girls. The trip back home from the hospital was mostly quiet. The silence broken only by occasional sniffles as her daughters worked to keep in their tears. Cat felt immense grief and a kind of betrayal. Why was it that once she finally allowed herself to be happy, her joy was taken away?

She chose to go home and allow her miscarriage to happen naturally. She had medication for the pain, but it did little to sooth her aching heart. The emptiness she felt as the life slid from her body was unlike anything she had felt before.

Theo was mostly quiet, focusing more on Cat rather than expressing his own grief. They spent a lot of time alone, while together. Each allowing the process in their own way.

It took some time, but the pregnancy got Cat to thinking about the possibility of another child. She questioned the wisdom of it but she could not deny the fact that she would constantly feel this little spirit around her trying to come into being. It was as if the child she lost had been paving the way for the one who needed to be here.

She thought then about her ancestors. She thought about all of their stories they had been revealing to her. It was as if they had all been paving the way for her too. There was some reason she needed to live in this time and in this place and there was a reason for baby number seven, to join this family.

She was torn between trying for a baby once again or doing the 'logical thing' and quitting while she was ahead. Theo really wasn't much help in making the decision.

"Well, being an older mom, you'll need to get in shape." He stood up straight and flexed, "I can help you with that. It's gonna take a lot of practice." He winked at her and she rolled her eyes and playfully punched him in the arm.

"I'm serious. Do you think I'm crazy to even be considering this?"

"Of course I do, that's why I love you." He smiled then continued, "You know I love babies. I'm okay either way, this is really up to you."

Cat had scheduled an appointment with her doctor for a physical and to discuss the feasibility of another child at her age. But in the time between making the appointment and keeping it, she had finally made the decision not to have another child.

"Good Morning Catherine" the doctor entered the room.

"Good morning" Cat answered. "Look, I wanted to let you know I decided to go ahead and keep my appointment because I'm due for a physical anyway, but I decided against another pregnancy so that's one less thing we'll need to talk about today." She smiled feeling a bit relieved.

"Oh, I see." She glanced down at her chart. "Well, it looks as if someone else made their own decision about that too. You're already pregnant."

Cat sat there stunned. 'I should have known' she thought to herself. The spirit presence of this child was so strong there was no way she wasn't going to sneak into this world one way or another. All those weeks she had agonized over a decision she now felt was never hers to make. She smiled to herself. 'This one is going to be special. She's going to be strong. I can't wait to meet her' she thought.

It seems that the new baby was just as excited to meet everyone else as well and she made her arrival two weeks before her due date. She must have known it was important to come early. It was important for her to meet her father because not much past her arrival, he nearly left.

Theo had had triple bypass surgery after finding out that the sick feeling his doctors kept dismissing turned out to be heart attacks. The doctor casually called them 'widow makers'. Over twenty-five scar sites had been discovered on his heart and the doctors told her that a large portion of his heart was 'necrotic'. Doctor talk for 'dead'.

They rushed him to specialists following a stress test that Theo had finally convinced his doctor to give him. After the specialists realized how serious it was and they admitted him as soon as it was possible. Her older children stayed with the younger ones, each dealing with the stress of the unknown in their own way.

Cat left early the morning of his surgery with a last look at her children. She put on a brave face that belied the churning in her gut. She told them with an encouraging smile that she would keep them informed while she silently prayed that he would indeed come back home to them all. She couldn't lose him again.

His surgery was successful but his recovery was long. He spent more time than they thought at the hospital and once home, she felt helpless to do anything for his pain. It took months before he would begin to feel semi-normal. His health had set them back financially, but it put them ahead as far as their relationship was concerned. They grew closer and more determined to not waste time pursuing anything other than a magical life.

Meanwhile, Theo and Cat worked tirelessly on finishing the old house. What had once been a worn down and filthy college student frat house had been restored inside and out.

Both Cat and Theo were muralists and faux painters and the rental property, was finally being restored to its former glory. They had even faux painted all the trim to look like real wood again. The work they put in not only made it a better place in which all of them could live but because of it, their landlord gave them a break on rent.

Cat loved being home and looked forward to the evenings when all the kids were finally in bed. She and Theo would quietly slip under the covers themselves. Her favorite thing was to be close to him. She would lie next to him, her head on his chest, his arm wrapped around her, skin on skin, listening to his new heart.

It was the only time she ever felt completely at peace, safe and loved. It was then that she would often ramble trying to connect the various dots and knowings that would come to her unbidden. "Did you remember to set the alarm? We have an early morning at the market tomorrow."

"I did." Cat mumbled as sleep began to creep in. "Oh, also, our landlord is going to stop by tomorrow evening. I guess he has a friend who is looking to get into the rental property business and he wanted to show him the house." she added.

"Okay. I'll make sure the kids help to neaten up before then."

She was lost in thought a long time but as her mind finally began to calm down, she whispered, "Theo?"

"Yeah?" he mumbled.

"What if we are the Goddesses?"

He put his arms around her. "You are."

"No. Really. What if they are just imaginary and we are the real thing?"

"Like a mirage?"

"I guess…"

"Did you know that the word for mirage is 'Fata Morgana'?"

"Wait. Like Morgan La Fae?"

"Yes. Sort of…" He held her tighter. "Mirages aren't imaginary. They're just reflections that are beyond our horizon. Morgan la Fae is one of the Fates, the Fata or Morae."

"So, the Fata, the Fates are just beyond the Horizon?"

"Yes, always just beyond… but some can see their reflection. The Morae rule the Fae." She could feel him smile. "That's you."

She smiled. "And the Wormwood Queen?"

"Nah, she is beyond that. She is of the Horae. Fée Viridi. The more ancient ones. The Yoruba call them the 'Iyaami Osoronga' or 'Our Mothers from the Stars'. The Wormwood Queen is the one who returned in the Green Age. The Age of our heart."

"Wait… She returned? What age is this then?"

Theo pointed to his crotch and she laughed. "No, seriously. Follow me." He pointed to his chakras as he went up. The Red Age of the Great-Unknown Grand-Mothers. Then…", he touched his womb." …the Orange Age of Grand-Mothers." He touched his belly. "The Yellow Age of Women…" Then he touched her heart. "This, then, became the Age of Great-Grand-fathers, the Green Age. Where Dice re-emerged but went into hiding. She is your

Wormwood Queen. Dike, Justitia, Virgo, I call her the StarMaiden. She is in every culture."

"What Age are we in now?"

He traced up his chakra line again. "Red is 5,000,000 years of the Unknown Primacy. Orange is 500,000 years of Grand Matriarchy. Yellow is 50,000 years of Matriarchy. Green is the 5000 years of Grand Patriarchy like Monotheism, Linear thought and Misogyny where the Fae go into hiding." He left his heart and touched his throat. "Blue is the 500 years of Patriarchy we call Discovery but everyone else calls it the Genocide, about the time of Columbus. Age of Discovery lasts till about 1962 when Kennedy is assassinated, like the death of Camelot and Patriarchy. You are born in the 50 years of the Indigo Age 'The Age of the Children'." he said touching his third eye. And our daughter is the last of your race before we entered into the Ultra-Violet Age in 2012. The Age we are in today. The Age that marks the beginning of the new cycle of '5's in reverse."

Cat had a sudden memory and traced up her own chakras and repeated a memory to herself, "5000 years, followed by 500, by 50, by five…" She touched her crown. "…and then today!" She repeated a memory. "…But the GrandMothers would return if the Children were in danger…" She gasped at her memory and turned to Theo but he was fast asleep, snoring like a hibernating bear. Had he been asleep this whole time? She shook him. "Hey! Wake up!"

"Cat?"

"Tell me those ages again?"

"Ages? What ages?" He mumbled. "I don't need no stinkin' ages…" He snored again.

"Hm?"

He mumbled "I love you."

"Theo?"

"Hm?" He was asleep for sure.

"So, you're saying I'm not a goddess?" She said to herself. She thought...

"Horae are goddesses too. Go to sleep..."

She didn't know how to take that so she 'googled' it and smiled.

When she finally settled down, she began to wonder if this conversation had ever actually taken place. Then her mind went to wondering what the word 'actually' actually meant. Theo's snoring seemed to be lulling her out of her head. She put her arm around her sleeping bear and whispered, "I love you."

CHAPTER 36

The sleep she slipped into, however, was an uneasy. Her mind was too full of thoughts, ideas and concerns and morning came all too quickly. They were going to go to the new and improved farmer's market meeting about having winter hours. It would be a real boon to their business to go year-round.

Cat went to the meeting on her own however, as Theo had decided to stay home with their new baby. It was too cold of a day for him to be out yet so soon after heart surgery and he wanted to start a batch of their most expensive and popular spice curry that contained over twenty-five organic spices.

At that meeting, they announced their new manager and she approached Cat afterward. Cat was happy to see her old friend who had previously owned the funky cool women's clothing store right next door to Cat's shop. She, too, had been forced out of business just before Terra Stella had to close.

"Hey, I know you guys work under the Cottage Laws and all so I thought that I would give you a heads up. The board is saying that the state wants you to carry insurance for us separately and prove that you have a matching 5-million-dollar coverage for yourself as well." She knew that she was carrying bad news and that there was more.

So did Cat. She cringed before asking, knowing that Shauna was just being a good friend and trying to do her job.

"There's more. Isn't there?"

Shauna looked at her and handed her the new application for the Winter and following year. Cat read it and winced in the first two paragraphs.

"I'm sorry." Shauna already knew that she had just handed her a death sentence.

The previous governor, a woman, had created a 'cottage industry' law that had created over 900,000 jobs, mostly for women just after their store had closed. After the recession that had killed both of their stores, the new governor created new laws to kill the Cottage Industry as well.

Cat looked at the insurance requirements and noticed three proofs were needed. They would be forced to rent or own a licensed separate kitchen a licensed and insured storage unit onsite and insure every single market where their goods were sold.

Cat grew more upset as she read on. They would not be able to have children in the licensed facilities or store anything at home. The spices and teas they currently had would not be usable. They would all need to be purchased new and opened in front of a licensed inspector.

There would be no more cottage industries at any 'cottages'. Or anywhere else. This was more than a death sentence. It was the actual execution. Cat went home to tell Theo, already in the midst of making a single curry they sold that had over twenty organic herbs and spices in it.

"So basically, they are telling us it's still legal for us to make this but there is no place that will allow us to sell it." Theo looked at the investment that they had in just this one product they sold.

"Basically. Yeah." Cat looked at him. "Except we need to dump every spice, every herb, every tea and buy all new. And no 'grandfather clause' to save our stock of already made stuff…"

"I guess you have to be a grandfather for that." It wasn't funny but it was true. The law only 'grandfathered' businesses created before the women's 'Cottage Law'.

Theo wasn't about to quit and suggested that they look into what it would take to continue. He had heard that a commercial kitchen had opened up nearby that was designed just for these new laws and they had the older kids look after the babies as they drove over to a spot near their old store to check it out.

Once back in the old neighborhood, they noticed how so much had changed. All of the woman-owned stores they once knew were being replaced with medical and insurance places and the like. The old yarn shop, women's coffee shop, yoga studio and other funky friendly places were being 'gentrified' by professional offices and upscale eateries. Mostly owned by 'gents'.

They walked into an old closed restaurant that had been converted to a leasable, shared commercial kitchen. It was time to see what their new reality may entail. By the time they returned home that evening, Cat was sick with worry. The trip had been a bust, their costs would be ten times what their overhead was now. The next morning Cat and Theo got right to work to see how they still might be able to comply with the new food laws. They had not given up hope but it was hard for her to focus.

"This sucks!" Cat began. "No matter how we pencil this out, it doesn't make financial sense. Not only would we have to rent the space, but we would have to rent the storage there. We'd also have to buy completely new inventory, to be delivered, opened and stored there! We just don't have that kind of investment!

Most of all, we can't be with our children and work at the home we worked so hard at restoring for us and the business." It was like a door had closed and Cat had one of her head tingles that seemed to be a warning. "I have a bad feeling." Was all she could say before their doorbell rang.

It was their landlord and he was with his friend. They were finishing up their beers and the last of their cigarettes as they admired the koi pond, swale and natural garden Cat had so lovingly created to solve a drainage problem.

"Wow! You guys have really fixed this place up! It looks amazing!" He exclaimed upon entering.

Their landlord spent some time listening to Cat and Theo talk about what they had done to the place. She showed off the day porch that had previously been unusable but was now converted to two more bedrooms. They lead him to the basement where, through loads of hard work, they had created three more bedrooms. Cat thought she was sharing something she was rightfully proud of. Theo had been a set designer and they both were faux painters and the house that was nearly slated to be condemned was now a model showplace for their many skills.

She began to feel uncomfortable though, as she watched her landlord take in all the changes they had made. She wasn't sure why, but she didn't like the vibe she was picking up. The 'friend' didn't seem to be asking the kind of questions he should be and their landlord was acting strange.

The very next day was December 1st. Cat opened an email from him to find what their new rent would be when their lease was up in January. He wrote that now that the house was what it was, he needed to charge for all of the livable spaces they had created. He didn't elaborate but said to call him on his cell phone. Cat didn't like that because he only used that number when he didn't want his wife to know where he was or what he was up to.

When Theo called instead of Cat, their landlord seemed relieved. He took the approach of acting as if he had a problem with which he needed their help. It seemed his former baseball player fraternity that had previously rented the house Theo and Cat were currently living in, had pretty much destroyed it. Their landlord, and fraternity alum, had to evict them. However, he had promised them that once it was restored, he would let them move back in.

The team practiced right across the street and could not miss all the work that was being done. He apologized and said that he hadn't thought that it all would be done so soon.

The 'friend' who had visited was a baseball frat brother who lied about why he wanted to 'see inside the old place'. When he saw the pond in the yard, the gardens, the wood work and all of the rooms restored and legal for a dozen people, he decided the fraternity should have it back. Immediately.

They were offering several hundred dollars per room and Cat and Theo had created the possibility of ten rooms. He made it sound like he had no choice unless they could match the offer. It was more than three times what they were paying. They couldn't afford it and would be forced to leave.

It seems the good job they did at fixing the place up was a little too good. Of course, they could sue if they could afford a lawyer but he reminded him, the fraternity had lawyers too. He basically said that his loyalties had to be for his 'buds and bros' and he would fight for them, because they had money and they 'had his back'.

Cat heard about his phrasing and wondered if he knew that the whole phrase was 'Buds and Bros over Bitches and Hoes…'

Cat fought to keep it together. She fought to understand why all of this was happening. Her dreams only served to scare her more lately. She was unclear of the lessons she was supposed to learn. She had no clue as to the direction she should take. She felt desperate and fought the urge to sink inside of herself and to shut everyone else out.

She closed her eyes to the world before her even as she feared the world that she would enter when she slept. She just repeated over and over 'Teach in Her Name. Heal in Her Name. Bless in Her Name' as she fell into another dream filled night that she knew would be worse than her day.

CHAPTER 37

Cat was now pretty used to opening her eyes and looking at her hands to see who she was or where she was in her dreams that seemed to happen nearly every night now. This time, she knew she was somewhere different, someone different. She struggled painfully to move and found it impossible to raise arms in front of her as she wanted to. They were manacled behind her in iron too heavy for her frail hands.

She had the sense that this was not just to imprison her but to keep her from praying. A man at a table looked at her as she sat on the floor, He walked towards her and offered her water from a tin cup. She looked away. He poured a trickle on the ground in front of her. Getting no reaction, he threw the rest at her face.

She knew the Archbishop quite well from their many battles as he fought to take her Monastery into his control. She knew him from even before that when he had been a newly appointed bishop who had sent her husband away because he thought he could then have her. Their history was filled with his attempts to 'know' her and vent his anger when he could not have her in the ways he wanted.

Although she was now protected by Rome, it was a former acolyte, who had been excommunicated, who had turned on her. Offering the Archbishop a final attempt at revenge. This was supposed to be a trial but she had never heard of anyone being declared innocent. Especially since she and the new Archbishop had 'history' that had never settled in his favor.

He adjusted his miter and intoned gravely, "You, Mother Abbess Lavieauna Akaterina Marie de la Motta are accused of consorting with the devil and of witchcraft. I am here to take your testimony and plea.

"You are charged with causing a pox on the people of Lausanne and a plague with your poisons. If you plead guilty, we will proceed to your confession and sentencing. If you plead innocent, we will proceed to trial. This will be your sole testimony.

"We will ask you questions and you may speak until you are finished or until I tire of your testimony and decide that it is no longer relevant. Do you understand?"

Cat felt herself nod and she ached in every tiny fragile joint of what seemed to be a very old body. She opened her eyes to look down on her feet that were swollen as if they had been broken. She nodded again through the pain.

"You must answer in words."

"Yes, your Grace."

"Are you a witch?"

"No, your Grace."

"Are you in consort with the Devil or one of his demons?"

"No, your Grace."

"Are you a sister of the Dominican Nunnery at Motta d'Dea, north of our canton?"

"Yes, your Grace."

"Are you aware that your order was declared heretical since your Sisters' defection from St. Chiassez?"

"Yes, your Grace."

"I can end this inquiry right now with that admission. Do you wish to recant?"

"If I may, your Grace, I will remind you that we were reinstated with the Friary of Teaching Brothers at Motta d'Dea upon receiving Sanctuary from Rome and are protected as long as we stayed within those walls..." She couldn't help adding, "...as you well know."

"You are now outside those walls." He bit back. "As you well know…"

She looked up at the Archbishop knowing that this was considered insolent but she did it anyway and spoke.

"Your Grace, you cannot kidnap, remove a person from Sanctuary. I will answer your questions and you may decide whether it is a confession or my last testimony. You intend to kill me either way and I am too old to plead for my life, so I will plead for you to tell the truth instead. I invoke my right to an advocate as a Soldier of Christ." She looked directly at the scribe now who was looking at the Archbishop as if to ask if he should record what she had just spoken.

The Archbishop fought the instinct to punish her for speaking so but he was under orders from Rome to treat her with deference as the people of the Lausanne Valley and even the neighboring Cantons, all considered her to be a living Saint and the Prussians were looking for any excuse to invade. Her use of the Latin term also meant that she knew her rights to being interviewed by Rome as he really had no jurisdiction over her order or the monastery.

The Counter Reformation was losing power in the South as the Church was unable to stop the smallpox and outbreaks of the plague. He was under strict orders to put her on trial or release her alive and unharmed. His men had already been reprimanded for breaking her feet. They said she had resisted and broke her own feet.

"Very well, if you are intent on rambling, I will bring in a scribe as soon as Rome deems to send us a solicitor that speaks your Egyptian tongue." She understood his gibe at her Sinti ancestry that the Romans called 'Egyptsienne' or just 'Gypsy'.

"I speak Latin. If you unchain me, I will write it myself… She paused and bit off the remaining, expected honorific. "…your Grace."

The Archbishop turned his back on her and waved at the jailers to open her cell for him to leave. As soon as she could no longer hear his footsteps, she passed out from the pain.

Cat was disturbed as she realized who this was. Somehow, the cute little baby that had first arrived days after her birth to Motta had grown to be this old lady now accused of witchcraft. She was also the one who owned the bakery, became a nun and, now, here she was.

She was also the Mother Abbess of Motta. As Cat struggled to wake from what could only be a bad ending, she was suddenly overcome with a sense of peace. Had she died? No, she could hear the old woman beginning to hum and as she hummed, she had fleeting glimpses of happier times.

She 'saw' her happy childhood at the fort as if it were her own memory. Her mother and father had grown old there and were remembered for their goodness, their devotion to their elixirs and to each other. She saw her wedding to a soldier in Geneva and his death in her family chapel in Neuchatel Principality.

LaVieauna raised her daughter with the help of the nuns and, eventually, took her vows. She also initiated into the secret sisterhood that had practiced in the caves since time immemorial.

She was given the name of 'Aikaterina' for the saint who was a nun allowed to roam without sanctuary. LaVieauna was in the former monastery under the laws of Sanctuary and had not left since she returned to take her veil and vows.

At a certain point, Cat could not see what happened to the daughter but she could see that the nuns had a tenuous relationship with the Church in Geneva who considered them heretics after the 'Split at Estavier'. But the people overwhelmingly sided with the sisters and Rome needed to keep Catholicism the dominant religion in the South cantons.

Sister LaVieauna knew that the Reformation would gladly accept her and the entire rural peoples would join her. The hill people had been disease free for as long as the Sister's family had provided free Elixirs and taught them how to make bier and ale.

The rural Catholic 'alewives' were long a part of the women of caves and so were Helvetians, Paganis, Ethanikos, Juden, Sinti Roma and even Byzantium nuns that had fled from Turkish Bulgar regions a hundred years before. They associated and met informally at the market originally established by Aione. Secretly, each had six representatives and a 'hive' of their own that met in the Sanctuary on the full moon of every month unless there was a holy day in one of the hives.

Cat could feel LaVieauna remembering her life to keep calm. Memory and Song were her prayer. She had nothing left to ask for but peace and she knew that she would get it, one way or another.

Cat heard the familiar hum of the mead makers that Vanos' mother had intoned. She also recognized the Lutin's blessing that Aione played on the Lute to soothe the baby at night. Cat felt that she should somehow be comforting the old lady about to be burned at the stake but, instead, it was she who was being comforted by the old, broken and doomed memory of a nun who was now humming the old Hildegarde Von Bingen 'Ave Maria'. The sound of it seemed to echo as if the Sister was singing it in the Sacred Caverns.

Several days later, a Church Solicitor had had her chains removed and her feet were bandaged. She was sitting upright and they were trying to get her to eat.

"I will eat it cold. Let us finish. If it pleases your honor."

He bowed low. "Please, call me Paxtus. I am the Solicitor and Church Historian in Geneva and I have been told that you wish to exercise your right to testify and have a tribunal decide whether it is testimony or a confession. Is that correct?"

"Yes, your honor."

"Very well, I have taken the liberty of writing in your name, the charges against you and you have elected to swear upon your bible." He went over to a table and picked up three ancient leather wrapped books and raised an eyebrow. He knew he could not open them but he wondered why there were three and why they were under Holy Seal. He administered the oath and had her bibles remanded to her possessions that were being claimed by her daughter who had traveled down from the Benedictine Monastery at Monruz to pick up her affects and witness her sentencing.

After she swore on her 'bibles' the Sister was given water and helped to sit up in her bed. "Are you ready, Sister"

Sister LaVieauna rather liked the Solicitor. He had the same formal bearing as her long dead soldier husband and, like him, bowed often and spoke with a respect for, both, her and the law. "Your Honor, I am ready."

"Very well…" He nodded at the scribe who read the first question.

"You are accused of worshipping demons in their familiars as a bear, a bee and a pagan mother Aisatta. What say you?"

LaVieauna straightened. "Let me begin with the last. 'Aisatta' as you call her goes by many names and, certainly, wherever this Church has gone they have seen her by many names but despite the Church's objection to her color, Mari, the manifest 'Love of God' is an ancient and universal sacred and reverent image of the Mother of God we call Mari who is the Mother of Our Lord." She knew that the scribe would spell that last phonetically as Mary.

"We do not worship the bee and we do not associate it with the devil. Instead, many of our parishioners are Ethanikos from Greece and, by law, are entitled to practice their customs and Catholicism. We celebrate their feast day of St. Haram Al Bey who is their patron of Honey, bees and protector against the plague.

"Rome forgets that it is pledged to uphold the pact between the Byzantine Orthodox Churches as long as they are practiced by the peoples of that place. It also forgets that Romans are freely allowed to celebrate the feasts of Melona twice a year."

She paused to let the Scribe catch up. "When I say 'That place', I also remind his honor that the people of the Bernstadt also worship amongst us and we respect their customs especially their veneration of the bear but no one within our sphere of influence worships any animal or graven image." She looked at the scribe to see if he was finished.

He looked at the solicitor who had no questions and nodded for him to continue. The Scribe looked at the written question and blushed. "You are accused of the crime of Sapphic Lust and Sodomy. What say you?"

"I am quite innocent of engaging in anything but celibacy since my vows and I am certain that there is no law that describes 'Sapphic Lust' and I am quite incapable of Sodomy." The Solicitor turned away to hide his smile and the scribe hoped that the solicitor would not cross examine. The solicitor just nodded for the next question.

"You are accused of poisoning the waters of the lake and have been seen pouring your elixirs, extracts and libations into Lake Geneva. What say you?"

LaVieauna had never poured anything into that lake but she had poured any number of things into the stream that emanated from the cave spring that let into the lake. She decided that she could just deny this but she decided, instead, to indict the people of Geneva.

"Your honor, our sisters for many years practiced science as taught to us by Dr. Leandro Henriod-Motta a scientist and alchemist who studied in Basel at the University. He taught us that it is the dumping of human waste, feces and urine that attracts the things that spread the smallpox and plague.

"I submit that amongst my parishioners there is not a single case of Pox or Plague in all the years I have been Abbess, a good thirty years now. Tens of thousands have died in your parishes and Archdiocese and I have never left Sanctuary and would not do so to poison people who are already poisoning themselves."

The Solicitor was silent. He looked at the Scribe who averted his gaze at the counter indictment.

"You are accused of consorting with nymphs, sylphs and other unnamed elementals that are of the Devil. What say you?"

"I say that Lutins, Nymphs, Sylphs and any other names for the unseen people are recognized by no less than Paracelsus your father of Medicine and a Catholic. But further, I resent your inserting a claim necessary for my confession that seeks to satisfy the 'Malleus Maleficarum' as a proof that I am a witch.

"You realize that there is no Witch religion, no Heathen religion and no Pagan religion. Those are your warring Churches' names for women who defy your mastery. Linking it to Demons and Devils is your way of making anything I do or touch as 'witchcraft' because that is where you are going with this."

The Solicitor bristled imperceptibly but nonetheless. "Are you denying the existence of witchcraft?"

"I am denying your right to equate the workings of women as witchcraft and I am quoting this as a defense and an indictment of what you are trying here and trying to get away with here" She quoted from memory, 'Whether the belief that there are such beings as witches is so essential a part of the Catholic faith that obstinately to maintain the opposite opinion manifestly savours of heresy.'

Your Honor, this is the very first sentence of the 'Malleus Maleficarum' by Henricus Institoris, and I am making no claims about the existence of Witchcraft and, I assure you, that I am no rube or illiterate either. I am charged with witchcraft, a crime for which you have no definition but the arbitrary power to judge its existence and label anything I do as witchcraft. In fact, anything that you cannot understand, own, profit from or control you may call witchcraft."

The Solicitor was about to ask a question but knew that the tribunal would have a difficult time convicting a woman who would be reciting the litmus test for witches to them. He decided to end the questioning. "Do you have any closing statements Sister?"

"I am told that the charges against me include such things as the making of bier, the use of gall, to the making of Absinthe and the Elixir of Life. I deduce that you do not dare ask me about this because you know my defense. I will show you how this and other Churches have delighted to steal these things for their own and, so, how can they be the works of Satan when you intend to give these 'crafts' to men for your guilds and monasteries for profit."

He looked at the Scribe. "Answered but not asked. Strike that last response. Note that we are done here. This is the whole of her testimony or confession. The tribunal will decide. "Sister LaVieauna, I have decided that I am to be your solicitor, your 'Devil's Advocate, so to speak. Your appearance, tone and contrition will or will not be noted as part of my testimony on your behalf. We are done here." He saluted her by pounding his heart and revealing a tattoo. He had been a slave before becoming a Christian. It made the old Abbess feel sorry for him.

As he left, Sister LaVieauna heard a voice say, 'Teach in Her Name, Heal in Her Name, Bless in Her Name'. She crossed herself and took out her little black jet goddess. She stroked the figurine in her long gray hair that had not seen the light of day since she shaved it off a lifetime ago. As she touched it to her chest, she felt the spark jump from her heart to the figure for the very first time.

She held tightly to the beads in her makeshift rosary and waited for her daughter to be allowed to say goodbye. She heard the voice again as if it were a hundred voices in a hundred ages. Teach in Her Name. Heal in Her Name. Bless in Her Name.

She realized in that moment that she had said nothing in her defense to claim her devotion to the Mother. Her defense had been a denial and she prayed that the Mother would forgive her for protecting the thousands of women of the hills who would die if she had admitted the Heresy.

She hoped and prayed that 'Teaching, Healing and Blessing' would be able to continue if she also Died in Her Name.

This was the second time that Cat awoke with the smell of burning hair in her nostrils and smoke stinging her eyes. Her skin still felt as hot as it did when her soul left her body.

ABSINTHE, ALEWIVES & ALCHEMY

CHAPTER 38

It wasn't feeling much like Christmas that year. They were packing instead of decorating and trying hard not to panic as the days ticked by and they still had nowhere to go. Cat took her youngest children to the store to pick out a little Norfolk Pine to use as a Christmas tree that year as she knew it would be too much to set up hers only to take it down a week later to move.

She let her son pick out a topper for it even as she wondered how that would affect their finances. As she held the baby, she wondered how her first Christmas would be and realized that the baby would have a birthday just days later. Then her brain added '...and just days before we get kicked out of here.'

She had been trying to hold it all together and, in doing so, was withdrawing. Some of the older kids had already moved out and while that was easier and simpler than expected, it added to her sense of having failed them and drove her even deeper inside herself and away from Theo and their remaining children. It did not help that Christmas was her favorite season and that she had not a single present to give this year.

Theo was not one to shy away from saying what he felt or thought and his way of holding it together was to talk. He waited as long as he could and when he finally did say something it was not the way she had feared it. Of course, he was firm and impassioned but he was that way about everything. In fact, he was weirdly calm.

He didn't have any answers either as they faced no prospect of finding a home with no money, no car and no jobs as the market and other side jobs had disappeared while other people were enjoying the holidays. It seemed like their talks, however, were just making them feel worse.

"You know," Theo said "the only thing we haven't tried is magic."

"Magic." She spoke the word with more than a certain amount of cynicism. She had little faith in anything anymore much less magic. But as the thought coalesced in her mind she paused and whispered, "...magic..." She remembered her dream when she was told to 'Use your magic' the words rushed back into her consciousness. 'Teach in Her name. Heal in Her name. Bless in Her name.' Then she saw Isis, staring hard at her, willing her to put the pieces together.

"God damn it" she thought. Remember. It was time to remember what was dismembered.

She knew Theo worked magic in his own way. He was a Yoruba Priest and had lived with the First Nations and had his altars, his pipe, drum, and he loved to cook for his ancestors and leave offerings that always seemed beautiful and magical. But she looked at all of her spiritual stuff that she had collected over the last few years and they didn't seem magickal at all. It just seemed like left-over inventory from Christmases past.

She thought about what she could do and had to be honest about what magic really was. What really worked? What she remembered, she realized was that it was not a 'what' but a 'who'. She suddenly knew just who she needed to talk to. She just didn't know how. She felt sure, however, that if she could reach them, they would give her guidance.

Sometimes, while sleeping, and, more recently, when she was awake, she'd caught glimpses of another place and another time. She was pulled to go to that place now. To find 'Her'.

Sometimes she would have visions where she would see herself at the edge and just outside of a group of older women. It was always night. Sometimes there was a fire, but its light didn't make it any easier to see. Their faces were always obscured by the darkness.

Sometimes one or two of them would break away to talk with her. Sometimes they ignored her, but allowed her to stay and watch their ceremonies. Sometimes there was drumming, or a kind of thrumming. It was comforting like a heartbeat. They were always discussing things, planning and sometimes it seemed, plotting.

She had the sense that there were a few of them who were 'assigned' to her. They all knew when she was there, but only a small group of them would engage with her. They were the same ones each time.

Running purely on intuition, or maybe it was desperation, Cat decided to create an altar and talk with them now. She grabbed an empty square box, some black table cloths, her crystal skull, candles and offerings. She felt pulled to add piles of dirt and bones to her altar as well. She chose a few special river rocks and put those out too.

She took them down to a now empty bedroom in the basement. She thought about a time, not that long ago, when she would never have ventured to that part of the house by herself. Maybe she was becoming braver, she thought, or maybe she was just becoming desensitized with one thing after another hitting her so hard. She decided it didn't matter. She had work to do.

Once everything was set up, she lit the candles and closed her eyes. The strong smoke of the sage she burned wrapped around her in the darkness. She took a deep breath, exhaled and waited. Nothing. She waited a bit more and finally got up and sat in an old office chair her son had left when he moved out days before.

Once away from the altar, she wondered if maybe she was doing it wrong. She held her smudge stick and sniffed its pungent burnt end and noticed the cedar wrapped around it. It reminded her of the store but also of something else. Somewhere else. Someone else. Some time else…

Time seemed meaningless. Sounds dissolved into a thick quiet. She slowly opened her eyes, they were heavy and unfocused. She watched as a spider crawl across her altar made its way onto her crossed legs. "Hello Mama." she whispered.

She began to smell cedar and damp earth, she began to feel that she was not alone in the room. She shivered, but not from fear. From far away she heard, "We are the ones who worshipped Her since before time. She has always been. We have always been…"

She stepped, barefoot onto the cool ground and faced two women who stood before her. One was covered with a bearskin with the head still attached giving the appearance of three faces instead of two, looking at her from darkness.

"I need help." was all that she could think of to say.

They looked at each other for a silent moment and turned back to her, as if she was understating the obvious. She tried to say more but as she looked at their faces they would change. morph and show themselves as different people, both men and women, in her many lives she had dreamed.

The woman in the bear-skin spoke. "Remember" was all she said. The other woman, patiently turned toward her but Cat's attention was focused on her wrists. They were tattooed. They were tattooed with what Cat knew, somehow, to be stars.

The one with the bear skin motioned to the cave wall and she saw animals drawn with ochre, umber and other earthy colors; the same palette she used in her own paintings. She walked closer to the walls and the animals painted there began to move. She had the sudden understanding that they were stars, constellations migrating to where they were now in her own time.

She looked up and saw a small cluster of stars and she drew a hand around it and one of the 'seeds' that was in that hand fell and fell as the hand faded away.

The hand image receded into the darkness and it was replaced with an image of the seed growing into what she realized was the earth shifting and moving with heaving breaths. Cat was being moved along with it. The ground rolled in slow waves and she had no choice but to succumb and go along. And as she struggled for balance, she heard the words, "It's time to die."

A very old hand grabbed her own and placed it onto the cool cave wall. Someone else blew ruddy ochre dust all over it. When she removed it, she saw the stencil left alongside hundreds of others.

As she looked at her red stained hand it changed and changed again, becoming every hand that was hers before. She saw Vanos, LaVieauna, Melle and countless others. Now all dead.

"Oh shit." Cat said aloud as she opened her eyes and came back to the cool dark basement of a house that was no longer hers. "Oh shit." She repeated and then… "Here we go…"

She squeezed her eyes shut to see if she could go back to her magical dream again but, instead she saw images of Christmases yet to come, strange places and more loss. This was not the sunny silver lining and rainbow ending she had hoped for. This was more like the ghost of Christmas Future

CHAPTER 39

Cat had been so disturbed by her dream of Cécile's rape that she had not slept in a few days. One morning after the babies had gone down for their nap, she took a moment to rest as well and tried to understand why she had been feeling her familiar 'head tingles' all morning. She couldn't shake the strangest fear that someone was trying to kidnap her babies. She tried to tell herself it was a result of all the losses in other areas of her life and the fact that she hadn't slept in days, but she was unable to shake the feeling.

Baby Aikaterina Henriod de la Motta was born on the day that the soldiers had come through the Roma and Sinti villages looking for the 'Jennsiche Swaartzen'. It had been many years since a witch had been killed but the Swiss Prussians had decided that taking the babies of the Oublier was easier than killing them. The parents would eventually all die off and their children would be raised by Christians.

Aikaterina's mother had foreseen this, had warned their village. Many villagers had decided that she was a whore, not because they did not believe that she had been raped but because they knew, as a midwife and healer, she could have prevented the pregnancy. Instead she willingly birthed the child of her Roman Catholic rapist, a soldier at that and, therefore, could not be trusted.

Therefore, it was only a small contingent of 'wanderers' or 'Oublier' that set out for Saintes-Maries-de-la-Mer, a journey of over three hundred miles. Many of those going had originally come from there and had migrated when the Swiss Cantons and even the principalities were open and free to any religion. The Cantons in those days were also democracies where the wandering Oublier had hoped to become citizens and finally belong to a country. But that had been before the Reformation and Counter-Reformation. Even then, they had been blamed for the plague that had re-appeared.

Aikaterina's mother had descended from Sinti peoples who were related to these Gitanas. Her people were from Sicily and had migrated disguised as a Commedia dell'Arte troupe once numbering a half dozen wagons. They were a traveling carnival and sold medicines and tin wares to survive. Her mother, whose name was Cécile was called 'The Melissa' and, until she had become pregnant, was very respected in her countryside villages to whom she ministered. Now, only a couple dozen or so, mostly women and babies, followed her wagon to the coast of France and to the possibility of freedom and safety for their children.

The little caravan of women was not safe traveling alone so several rode horseback dressed as armed men. Cécile had also cast a small glamour helped by marking the wagons with the red cross and 'Rx' that indicated a house was being treated for smallpox or plague.

After many weeks, the women finally reached the coast. They were all welcomed, especially Cécile, who had brought medicines. It was not long before she was known for elixirs, her tea readings and her skill with the 'Asiette' a French word for both 'plate' and 'advice'. In fact, they often called her 'La Asietta'.

Among the many things she had brought with her in her little wagon was a square wooden box of her 'possibles', the objects she used for her altars, the box itself was a cubit. It had the symbols on each of the six sides that matched her other little square wooden box that held her 'Asiette' and she brought it as a place to put her Madonna Aisatta.

As she began ministering to the women of the town, they would come into her wagon and would bow low to her Madonna. Another curious thing was that they began clothing her statue. Bringing her cloaks, jewelry and crowns. She took this as a local sign of respect but when the local priest came to visit, he also brought her a cloak and he touched her feet just as the women did.

"Father, why do you venerate my idol like the Gitana?" She said it with as much respect as possible. "I thought you were Roman…"

"I am." He laughed. "But Sara La Kali is our most important saint here and I am Gitane by birth and Catholic only by persuasion."

"Is that what you call her here?" She was very curious now.

"Yes." Then he shifted nervously. "Actually, Rome no longer recognizes her or any of the Black Madonna's on the Camino."

"I call her Aisatta as my mother did."

"Ah… Well the Sinti would call her that. You see, she is 'Isis' to you, an old Egyptian goddess. That is why they call us 'Egyptienne' or 'gypsies'. But we are all, both of us, originally from India and so we see her as Tridevi. She is Saraswati, Lakshmi and Kali all in one. Sara, La, Kali"

"You are a veritable heretic for a priest, Father." She smiled and meant this as a compliment given her distrust for Catholics.

He bowed and held out his hand. "Come, I must show you…"

She did not completely trust him but, at the same time, she did. She decided she would follow and felt safer when, after a few minutes of a fast, silent walk, they arrived at the church. He took out a set of great keys and lead her inside. When he opened another door in the back, all she saw was darkness and she recoiled. "Where are you taking me?"

He understood her fear and smiled as warmly as he could. "My lady, you are quite safe with me. I am a heretic only because I have little desire for women." He winked and lit a torch from one of the altar candles. Its light revealed the stairs and as he descended, he said, "You are quite safe with an old sodomite."

She slowly followed and was stunned when she reached the bottom.

The father bowed low. "This, is the only lady in my life."

There, on a cubit, was a black Madonna covered in so many cloaks and so bejeweled that only her serene eyes reflected from her black face in the torch light.

"I do not know how you have come about yours but this is the Lady of the Three Maries. It is said that when the three Marys came to these shores, the boats could not get close enough to allow the women to safely reach shore. So She spread her cloak on the waters and they walked across never getting their feet wet."

Cécile bowed low to the statue only slightly taller than her own. She noticed the skull, bones and dirt that had been placed at her feet and she knew that this one was a guardian for the dead as well, just like hers. She looked at all the offerings on the black cloth around the cubit and saw that she was also the guardian for babies. Last she noticed the beautifully painted plates under the offerings.

"Quimper ware, Father? What happened to your vows of poverty?"

"You have a good eye, but I must confess that they are counterfeits, the work of a pilfering priest with too much time."

"You, Pere Andro?" She was impressed. "Would you teach me? Women are asking me for plates."

"I've heard about your plates…" He raised a teasing eyebrow. "I will teach you to paint in my poor peasant way if you bake me some Dirgelli Tarrochio."

Cécile blushed. The priest knew far too much about her. "Father, I must leave you before your parishioners kidnap my baby, but I thank you for showing this and your secrets are safe with me."

He bowed low and smiled. "I doubt that anyone here doesn't at least suspect that I… uh… paint, but we are not of Rome and Rome is not of us. I expect cookies soon…"

As she ran back to her wagon, she felt lighter, like something had just lifted and as she took little Kat from the neighbors, she noticed that her baby was wearing a little crown.

"This is beautiful, little one. Are you stealing jewelry now?"

Her neighbor bowed low. "I couldn't resist, Lady Cécile. Your Aikaterina belongs to the 'stars'." She pointed to her Tarrochio spread on the little tea table. "Look, even Hecate is Tridevi. She too, belongs to the 'Earth and Stars' if you take my meaning…" She said this as she bowed low but still looking up.

Cécile bowed low back. She suddenly realized she was being tested, talked to in code. The old woman was coding her. She bowed again, this time lower and touching her heart. "Terra Stella, my Lady."

The old woman beamed. "Terra Stella." she intoned back and then she added, "I knew it the moment I laid eyes on you."

As she walked back to her wagon, she sang the song of Inanna to her daughter and finished by blessing her feet.

"The moon under your feet." The baby giggled as she traced a smile on the feet that had escaped their swaddling. She tickled the little belly and touched the third eye below the little crown pinned to her curls. "Terra Stella."

As she stepped inside her wagon she bowed to her Madonna and noticed that she, too, had been given a new robe and a crown of seven, eight pointed stars, just like Kat. She also noticed that her new blue cloak was clasped by a beautiful bejeweled brooch in the shape of a honey bee.

As she cleaned and rewrapped her baby, she noticed that Kat had a smaller bee pinned in her swaddling. Cécile smiled. She placed the baby on her bed against the wall and crawled in beside her. As she went to sleep, she touched her own heart and head again without fear that she may be discovered. "Terra Stella." she whispered to her daughter and then she dreamed.

CHAPTER 40

Cat and Theo were about to lose their house during the worst December winter in a long time. Their van had died completely and she was driving a borrowed car on a slippery snowy day. They were broke and all she could think of was the children and Christmas. She didn't even know how to look past the fact that four days later would be the baby's first birthday and two days after that, they would be homeless.

Even as she drove in the slippery icy streets, she should have been paying attention but, instead, she was distracted and feeling panicked. She wasn't far from home but she decided to pull over immediately instead of driving one second more.

She stopped at the familiar dog park near their home and put the car in Park. Her heart was racing and she had the fleeting thought that she was finally going crazy. She turned off the engine and squeezed her eyes shut tight against the panic.

The images which had been playing in the background of her mind were now front and center. She saw the underside of a large dark wooden table and she realized that she was viewing it from the vantage point of a small child. She heard a voice that she knew to be her mother's, talking tersely to someone in high German and thought it strange to hear the language in which they learned their lessons, instead of the French her mother usually used.

It was forbidden for girls to learn Latin and too dangerous to teach them in French, which was not the language of the Counter-Reformers. It had not occurred to her that her mother could also speak the Prussian German just as it had not occurred to her mother that the little girl sitting under the great carved table could understand it from her schooling. Even stranger to the girl was to hear a Roman Catholic speaking it so fluently.

"Your Grace, you realize that by withholding my mother's personal affects, you are breaking the law."

"You think I care?" His voluminous robes could be seen to shift under the table. "I own you..." He said as he stood and held up a silver filigree locket that he squeezed as if he were crushing it, "...If it had not been for Rome, you would be a personal affect in my residence. What do you think will stop me from simply taking you right here and now like I did your mother?"

From under the table, the little girl saw her mother twist the leather cord that held her rosary a little tighter. She seemed to be counting the beads nervously but her hand stopped and relaxed when it reached the small jet-black figurine that was at its end. Her mother suddenly calmed and slowly rubbed the figure on the knee of her long woolen robes. The girl saw the ancient Archbishop step around the table and lean in to grab her mother. The little girl had the sudden and horrible vision of what was about to happen.

Without thinking, she grabbed her mother's rosary pendant and lunged from under the table. She touched the little figurine to the Archbishops heart. It sparked. The Archbishop straightened, clutched his heart and fell stone dead right in front of them.

Daughter and mother stood in shock and stared at the lifeless heap of robes before them. The child grabbed the silver locket that the Archbishop had still clutched in his giant hand. She did not know it as a fact, but felt that it belonged to her. It did.

Her mother grabbed her personal affects, pulled herself together and left out the door through which they came. She took her daughter's hand and walked calmly past the bishop, the Archbishop's Secretary. She nodded to him. "Camerlengo, you must attend to your duties."

The bishop was surprised to hear a woman not only speak Church Latin but she had just used the honorific of the 'Chamberlain' who must officiate over a dead Archbishop's death rites. With wide eyes, he ran in the office and, as mother and daughter walked out the great doors, they could hear the Bishop scream.

That scream was still echoing in Cat's head as she was startled awake to muffled yelling. "You can't sleep here, lady." An elderly man was peering into her driver side window. "This is a dog park. Sleep it off somewhere else." A large dog was also pressing his great slobbery jowls against the glass barking and she could hear his canines hit the window as he growled and lunged at her over and over again.

Startled, Cat shook her head and rubbed her eyes while quickly working to compose herself. "I… I'm fine, I just needed to close my eyes for a moment. Thanks…" she said, hoping they would go away. The old man looked skeptical and Cat realized that she must be 'a sight'. He continued to stare at her, for a moment not moving, but the dog seemed to get it and pulled the old man away and toward the fenced-in dog runs.

Cat stared at her slobber laden window and wondered how long they had been there. Then she thought about what she had just witnessed in her mind. The stories that had been unfolding over time, were rushing into her consciousness now all at once.

She had only a glimpse of the mother and daughter at the Archbishop's table and yet she, somehow, knew their entire lives.

She grabbed the steering wheel at ten-and-two and held on tight. "Get a grip, Catherine…" Something was happening. She could not stop it… She said it again as if the flood of memories, of dreams or whatever would stop if she said it with more intensity. "Get. A. Grip." As soon as she said "Catherine" she knew it was futile.

Catherine was no longer there. She was all of them. She was all of the stories. She was more than her one life, more than her one story. She rubbed her cold hands on the sleeves of her old wool coat with the fur collar and reached up to the rear-view mirror to see her reflection again.

A spark jumped to the mirror and she instinctively recoiled but her reflection reassured her that she was alright. She looked at her face and while she had, originally, wanted to check her make-up to make sure she didn't look as bad as she felt, she instead looked at herself and recognized something else. Someone else. Someone she knew long ago with wild hair and deep-set eyes that stared back at her through lifetimes and lifetimes.

As she readjusted the rearview mirror without redoing her hair or make up, she knew that she needed to get back home before this feeling left her. She needed to remember. What, she did not know but she needed to be home when it happened.

In her rearview mirror she noticed a car had stopped directly behind her blocking her ability to go in reverse. A man with two Dobermans was chatting with the driver. They both saw her back out a little but ignored her and went back to talking. Cat honked and the man with the Dobermans yelled something, gave her the finger and went back to talking.

"Fuck it..." Cat didn't think twice as she threw the car into Drive and drove over the snowy berm in front of her. She had 'Shit-to-do'.

ABSINTHE, ALEWIVES & ALCHEMY

CHAPTER 41

Cat was still freezing. Standing at the tall table Theo had made into a breakfast bar in the old kitchen, she was waiting for the kettle to boil as she carefully measured a teaspoon out of the last of her latest batch of Absinthe tea into her teacup from favorite antique teapot set. She needed to warm up after her time in the freezing car and she had not yet taken off her coat or boots.

It had been two weeks since they received the news that they must move. She had been looking at the beautiful black, butter and honey craqueleur cabinets that they had lovingly brought back from fifty years of frat house living and slumlord painting.

She stared into her tea cup and smelled the dried herbs awaiting hot water. She thought of her ancestors. Her dreams. She was just one ochre colored hand in hundreds, perhaps thousands, that had come before. That made her feel both small and infinite, simultaneously. She carried their dreams still, carried their stories and through them, in some way they became, she became, immortal.

They deserved tea. She grabbed a matching teacup and measured the herbs just as the water started to boil. She took off her gloves so she could feel the warm cup she was about to pour. She filled the ancestor cup first and slid the saucer to the tall stool opposite her. She no longer felt so alone. And she thanked 'Her'. Or maybe 'Them'? She pulled her seat out and almost sat on something. She set the boiling water down and picked up the package that had been opened and placed on the chair.

She flipped down the cardboard to read the package and it was addressed to 'Mademoiselle Isabella Cecile Henriott-DeMott'. It was for her new baby from her Aunt Henrietta, the one who had sent her the documentary. Cat had an idea what it was because she recognized the bubble wrap and careful Styrofoam packaging. It was Quimper ware.

Quimper ware was both of their passions. Not just Quimper ware but Henriot Quimper ware from Quimper France. The porcelain made by their shared ancestors. She and the ancestors were drinking from a Quimper tea set that her aunt had found. Cat carefully opened the Styrofoam case and she was right, the fine 'faience', country style painting, colors and the figures all pointed to her family's famous art. She carefully lifted it up and admired it.

She noticed it seemed different from the pieces she had previously come to know. It looked at first, like a typical Henriot Quimper but it was not round. It was hexagonal. There were six women painted on it in typical Breton dress of the Quimper style and region but they were each doing something different. There was a beehive in the center with three women on each side.

The floral design on the outside seemed a little too busy for her family's typical work but still in keeping with the stylized leaves and flowers normally portrayed. She immediately turned it over to look for the familiar 'HenRiot' signature or the initials 'HR'. But it was hand signed with a 'CHM' instead. So, she knew it was not the Poplar Beatrix often confused for a Henriot Quimper. But it was not a Henriot. As she turned it back over, she noticed something odd. There were hand-painted delft blue dots in clusters all around as decoration but they were not a part of the flowers.

She sat back down at her table, stared at the flowers and realized that the tall yellow ones were Artemisia Absinthium. She got excited as she guessed what this was. In short order, she identified five of the six flowers or leaves. They were the same ones she used in the making of her Absinthe tea. When she recognized the sixth one, she realized that she had found the missing herb. One that she had originally intuited but later discounted because she could not find it in any herb book as being in that region. But here it was.

She continued to stare at the plate. She noted that the blue dots that were in asymmetric clusters of 1-6 were like the six sides of an old-fashioned dice and she instantly knew that she was looking at an Asiette. A divining board, complete with a hive and all of the ingredients of Absinthe.

Her hands were shaking now so she gingerly put the plate down so as to not break it. She looked at the plate and wondered if she had a dice somewhere. But before she could go and look for one, she stopped to look at the beehive. The opening was in the exact center of the plate and painted an unusual black color for the style. She stared into the blackness and was drawn in.

The plate seemed to have been holding so much inside for so long that it was now spilling out. Into Cat. Too much and too fast to understand in a logical way but she was absorbing it nonetheless. It was all white noise and white light. It was coming so fast then suddenly, it stopped. The silence deafened. All went dark and the sounds of a carnival organ played in the foggy distance…

The old woman had every intention of going straight home. She still wore her theatrical make-up from the performance and the show was not even in its third act but who would miss her when they took their final bows? She had long crossed that line where she played ingenue roles to having become a 'character' actress.

To be honest with herself, she had long passed that bridge and her makeup was now to make her look younger on stage and not older so she had left it on. As she walked briskly and crossed the street to where it was more brightly lit. She noticed the light had come from Carnival lanterns festooning the wagons that had rolled into the park the night before.

She had to leave the theatre as soon as she was done with her little scene. Had to... She had read in the newspaper that day an account of the suicide of a young man who had killed his wife and family in a drunken rage that was blamed on Absinthe. It had occurred in Switzerland and it struck her that the article focused on the man's life and not on his murdered wife and children. She was particularly affected by this because she knew the man's father. He had, long ago, when he lived in Paris, raped her in a similar drunken rage. Evidently, the father had been drinking with the son and dropped him off home. It was there the son had killed his wife for not shining his shoes. He had been drinking all day but the paper blamed the two shots of Absinthe.

Seeing their names in print had triggered all the memories and had made it difficult to stay focused on the play. Thankfully, it was a minor scene and she took leave of the Stage Manager saying she felt ill. It was not a lie. As she walked, she took out the silver locket that had been in her family for many generations and held it tight for protection. And small comfort...

It had been rumored that her ancestors were witches and used it for spells. She was a bit skeptical about that legend but she still wore the empty locket since her daughter had died in a fire. She had given it to her daughter as a family heirloom, now it was hers again. She didn't believe in luck but she did find it comforting despite how it had come back to her. It was empty now but even that seemed fitting.

She slipped it back into her décolletage as she entered the busy park. The park was one of those little beautiful places left from the World's Fair of 1889 and she remembered how fifteen or so years before her entire city had been lighted and how the great tower had risen like a blazing phoenix to transform her city. She had been in love with the city the way she had been in love with the artists who had all loved and painted her. That was long ago. The day she had been raped was the day she closed her heart to Love. She had been walking her city of lights at night ever since. As if she were looking for someone. Perhaps herself.

She decided to walk through the park to see the attractions that brought Parisians out this late at night, partly to take her mind off of the news but also because she was feeling the need to stay in well-lit places. As an actress she felt a kinship with these 'gypsies' and smiled as she passed snake charmers, jugglers and a man in tights walking a slack rope with a shaky parasol. She thought of her younger days when she played young boys' parts in the theatre. She could juggle and even balance on a slackwire.

As she was about to turn out of the park to head home, she stopped, drawn by the lights of a little wagon parked on the grass slightly away from all of the others. This one was different in more ways than one. It appeared older and she recognized the beautiful painted 'lovers' and knew that this was a replica of a Commedia dell'Arte wagon from long ago. Exactly like one she had seen in a Romantic painting once.

Someone else must have known that very painting because here it was, reincarnated as the carny wagon of a fortune teller. The lanterns glowing outside shed light on an ornately painted sign that said, "Madame d'Motta Dea- She speaks truly and warns gravely - She knows all and tells all…"

She laughed at the sign's words. She could see the warm glow of lanterns through the open doors and she saw that the walls inside were beautifully painted with scenes and characters of old. Curious, she peered inside for a closer look. They reminded her of her younger days when she had been the 'Innamorati', and toast of Paris as well as the muse, and lover, of the most famous Impressionists and other Bohemians.

She admired the artist who had so skillfully reproduced this ancient wagon and wondered how it came to be. It did not match the more garish others and it was, oddly, set off from the main encampment. She climbed the little steps so that she could see the painted ceiling.

A little table and two chairs in front of a deep red curtain was the only furniture in the front of the wagon and she saw that the blue table cloth was finely embroidered with symbols and stars. Two cups of tea with tea leaves were set as if she had been expected. From behind the curtain she heard a rustling sound. Cat gasped as the curtain parted.

"Welcome. Step inside, I have been waiting for you, daughter." A woman's voice, with an accent she couldn't place emerged and poured them both hot water from a matching teapot and poured a little on a matching hexagonal plate.

"Excuse me, but do I know you?" Perhaps it was a fellow thespian from days gone by. The voice did sound oddly familiar. It was more than familiar to Cat. She was now looking at herself in the dream. Slightly more regal, way better dressed, but Cat was looking at herself coming out from behind the curtains.

The woman who looked like Cat motioned for her visitor to sit then continued to speak. "You do not know me but, of course, I know you. You are Paris Herself. The Lady in Blue. And while all may not remember, I still recognize you."

The woman was flattered. Who would have recognized her now? Now that she was no longer fair and her hair was graying and she was no longer the great beauty to whom the mysterious woman referred. "Forgive me, but I do not believe in the cards or such amusements but thank you for recognizing me. How did you know I would be here? Who are you?"

"S'il vous plaît, madame…" She indicated for her to sit again, bowed and sat herself as well. She lit a candle with the other candle on the table and held it over the plate. The actress saw that while the candle light showed that this was not anyone she knew, her hazel eyes shining back in the added candle light felt so familiar. She felt a glow from within her own eyes shining back at the woman as if she was just someone else's dream.

"Am I supposed to ask you questions or press some silver into your palms? How much?" She laughed nervously. She could ill afford a fortune teller.

The woman's smile put her at ease, "For you, dear one, there is never a charge and I know all of your questions, small and large, and all that has befallen you, good and ill, and all that will happen, if you so will…" She lowered the candle and placed her hands on the actress' hands, closed her eyes and, when she opened them, the woman suddenly felt as if she was now looking at someone else. Somewhere else. Some when else… The woman's head lowered and she stared intently at the beautiful hexagonal plate with a single dice floating, turning in the center looking like the last sugar cube at a tea party long since passed.

She looked up. The voice that spoke was not the same. As she spoke, the older woman suddenly felt odd and sighed as if a great weight had just been lifted. The woman seemed to look different, more magical, if that were possible, ageless, and her voice began to sing.

"You Sigh the Sadness, the Thousandth Sigh
The One you Loved has Long Gone By
She Sees you Now from the Other Side
'Tis She whose words you must Abide

And Space and Time are all a Blur
I speak for both, for I am Her
And this, my Riddle, if Truth is True
Is what, my Daughters, I Charge to You

There are no Cards, for me, no Redes
Salver and Cubit Serve my Needs
I speak to you Now in All of your Times
I am your Justice for All of Their Crimes

I tell you True, she died in the Flames
So She would not live to name all Their Names
She was lured to her Deaths by legions of Men
To ensure that she would not e'er Speak Again

And long long before her, before You and your Line
Before Sweet Lucretia and the Women Sabine
Our Kind was for Taking Again and Again
But this is the End of the Ages of Men

For I am the Dice and the Plate is my Mother
We come to Reclaim You in the Name of Another

I am Astraea, the Maiden of Scales
I See All that happened, I Know all your Tales

The Age of Injustice is nearing its End
And here, in your lifetime, I make this Amend
The Drink that was Drunk to murder your Child
I Reclaim for the Faeries who Live in the Wild

For I have come forth, the Fourth Fate Unseen
I am Viridi, the one that is Green
I am Pan's Queen, the Forest, my Palace
I am Justitia and Absent of Malice

Asherah, Ašratu, Aser-tu en Akkadia,
I brought the Ark to the hills of Arcadia
I am older than Yahweh, the One who's Unseen
I am young as the Springtime, the Wormwood Queen

I am the Maries, the Mari, the Aisatta
I am the last of the Horae, the Spring and the Fata
I am Sara and Lakshmi and Kumari Maa Kali
I am the An-Latta of Fatima Ali

And I am Herbes Sainte before they were Sainted
'Artemisia Absynthium' before it was Tainted
The Balm of the Bee, the Snakes Intertwined
I am Queen of Arcadia from Heaven Divined

And, yes, Pan is my offspring as are all of the Fée
Whether Green, Vert, Viridi I am all that they Say
And while I am not one of the Faerie Unseen
I am Fata Viridi, Yes, I am their Queen

For one hundred years they have stolen my Name
What once was of Women is now owned by Shame

But now it is ended their Time is at Hand
I reclaim Absinthe, from hence, it is Banned

And you, my fine Madame, will now start to heal
From Wounds of another I once named Cécile
But I called her Vanos and, before, Isabella
My Mother, her Terra and I am her Stella

And long before I was pushed from the Garden
Before I was labeled and left without Pardon
I was known as Lilatu the Maker of Charms
Who danced in the Moonlight with Snakes on my Arms

It was I who was followed after the Fall
It was I who left trails of Wormwood and Gall
And the Apple half eaten my Half of our Soul
For Adam still wished that He left me Whole

I arise from the Fountain, the Fatta of Springs
I speak for the Hora called Oracle Sings
And Absinthe will vanish a Hundred more years
No longer the Bringer of Death, Rage and Tears

Until Some One hears my Voice to Reclaim
And Calls to my Mother and My Holy Name
And remembers the Way of the Law and the Prophets
Forsaking the Taking and Making for Profits

If You can Remember as you Transcend your Strife
I, also, will bring you the 'Elixir of Life'
So this first is a Test that you must Complete
To unlock the Secrets, you have the 'Receipt'

And You who's no longer, a daughter of Eve
Will You heed my Riddle or Know, once you Leave,

Of what I am speaking and know that it's True
That Now I am speaking to the One who's in You

She, You, We are divided by Time
But the Love you seek is within this Rhyme
You will find Love, if that is your Goal
But first you must find your very own Soul...

With this, She stood up, bowed low and left while the actress sat there stunned. She, too, was about to stand but the smell of cigar and too much perfume assaulted her nostrils and forced her to sit back down as an old woman pushed aside the curtains. "Sorry you had to wait so long, I was taking a 'merde' if you catch my wind." She laughed at her coarse joke and the actress stared at her, stood suddenly and knocked over her own chair. The old woman ignored her as she went perfunctorily into her tired spiel. "I am Madame de Motta Dea... Gypsy Princess Extraordinaire..."

"Merci, Madame, there... has been a mistake, but... I must leave now, so sorry..." and she turned so fast she almost fell down the little steps. As she stumbled into the darkness, she had no idea what just happened, who the mystical woman was or what a single thing she said had meant.

But Cat did.

As the old woman walked away in a daze and clutched her little silver purse for comfort. She pulled it from her bosom she felt a faint spark as it passed her heart. It rattled oddly as she pulled it free and she saw through the filigree that something was inside. She opened it and gasped. It was the little jet Venus that had been consumed in the fire. She didn't understand how it could have returned...

But Cat did.

CHAPTER 42

She had no idea how long she had been standing there but her tea was still too hot to drink. Her tea. She thought, for a second to blame the Absinthe tea. But she had not yet had even one sip. Besides, the fabled hallucinatory properties, she had decided, were overrated. But as she looked at her cup of impossibly emerald tea, she realized that she had been doing it all wrong.

While she had been previously experimenting with the recipe using intuition, trial and error, she sat there now with the unshakeable knowing, the irrefutable proof that she not only knew which herbs really went in but, also, why, how much, when and more.

Of course, anyone could distill herbs common at the time and call it Absinthe as Perronoud, Ordinaire and Dubier all did but they had all failed and Cat knew why.

Now she knew the secret. She felt like she had solved a mystery. No. It was a Crime. She couldn't prove it but she could 'proof' it. She had already found the ingredients but now she had the prescription. She 'remembered' it. She knew exactly why they had failed and why his version would not cure.

But that mystery seemed to have been a trick to get her to 'do her destiny'. To 'remember'. It seemed oddly anticlimactic to discover the missing ingredient when she had also discovered that this was the end of The Age of Man. It was not her destiny to become another Mere Henriod. Her dreams had shown her thousands of years of crimes, rapes, murders, thefts, slavery and abuse. This was not about a magical elixir. Not yet. This was the beginning of something more. 5,555 years of patriarchy would not end with a secret recipe. There had to be more. The real mystery, memory and magic was just beginning.

She thought that she should have felt triumphant in that moment. She had solved a theft while uncovering a genocide. She had reclaimed a recipe but women were still not free. She had four daughters and the thought of losing a daughter like the woman in her dream was terrifying to her. It could still happen today. Was still happening today.

The Age of Man was not quite over. There was, as her friend Max had said, 'still shit to do'. Even in her own life she was being reminded that there was much work to be done. She thought about the alewives as she thought of 'still' shit.

Just recently, the cottage laws that had destroyed her own business were changed by the men in the state legislature. They were changed to allow men to make beer in their basement while she wasn't even allowed to make tea. She had not solved a crime. She had uncovered a conspiracy and it was not ancient history. It was still happening.

In that moment, she realized that there would not be anymore dreams. At least, not like she had been having since she first dreamed of Terra Stella all those years ago. She also realized what she had to reclaim. It was not just a 'recipe' but a way of life long lost and left by a long line of women. Women who were teachers before teachers were even a thing. Women who were healers before doctors existed. Women who blessed the world without wondering if they would be blessed in return.

She understood that this was not the answer to her financial troubles and her last 'dream' had shown her only too clearly that there would be more businesses, more houses, more cars, more money lost before she and Theo were out of the woods. Before everyone was out of the woods. She felt strangely calm about that. She felt as if she had been trying too hard to get 'out of the woods' when really, she needed to go back in. She knew what she must do.

She, herself, needed to learn more, heal more and bless more in order to do her Destiny. That was her next step. In 'Her' name. No books, no gurus, no paths would do this. She was a solitaire. A witch with no religion. She had no 'grammaire', no book of incantations except those from her dreams. What she had, what she had always had was Magic and Memory.

She must write a memoir, a grammaire, a grimoire, her own grimoire of Absinthe, Alewives and Alchemy. To Teach in Her Name. To Heal in Her Name. To Bless in Her Name.

Terra Stella…

ABOUT THE AUTHORS

Kate Henriott is the author of several books, including her popular 'Tea and Tasseomancy' and 'Talking to the Dead'. She is an award winning illustrator ('Energy Annie' series) and teacher to developmentally impaired adults. As the proud proprietor and maker of 'Mere Henriod's Extraite d'Absinthe', she continues to carry on a craft tradition stolen from her family hundreds of years ago... now reclaimed.

Ted Jauw is the author of many books including MythPunk thrillers 'The Fourth Choice', 'The Fifth World', 'Rescension' and the YA SteamPunk Thriller 'Teslation'.
The sequel, 'Teslation II', will be released at Teslacon 10.
Fall of 2019.

Ted and Kate have seven children and two grandchildren.

ABSINTHE, ALEWIVES & ALCHEMY

www.ingramcontent.com/pod-product-compliance
Lightning Source LLC
Chambersburg PA
CBHW030305080526
44584CB00012B/449